RAND | NATIONAL DEFENSE RESEARCH INSTITUTE

The Development and Application of the RAND Program Classification Tool

The RAND Toolkit, Volume 1

Joie D. Acosta, Gabriella C. Gonzalez, Emily M. Gillen, Jeffrey Garnett, Carrie M. Farmer, Robin M. Weinick

Prepared for the Office of the Secretary of Defense and the Defense Centers of Excellence for Psychological Health and Traumatic Brain Injury

This research was sponsored by the the Office of the Secretary of Defense (OSD) and the Defense Centers of Excellence for Psychological Health and Traumatic Brain Injury. It was conducted in the Forces and Resources Policy Center, a RAND National Defense Research Institute (NDRI) program. NDRI is a federally funded research and development center sponsored by the OSD, the Joint Staff, the Unified Combatant Commands, the Navy, the Marine Corps, the defense agencies, and the defense Intelligence Community under Contract W74V8H-06-C-0002.

Library of Congress Cataloging-in-Publication Data is available for this publication.

ISBN: 978-0-8330-5942-0

Preface

Between 2001 and 2011, the U.S. Department of Defense (DoD) has implemented numerous programs to support service members and their families in coping with the stressors from a decade of the longstanding conflicts in Iraq and Afghanistan. These programs, which address both psychological health and traumatic brain injury (TBI), number in the hundreds and vary in their size, scope, and target population. To ensure that resources are wisely invested to maximize the benefits of such programs, the Assistant Secretary of Defense for Health Affairs asked the RAND National Defense Research Institute to develop a set of tools to assist with understanding, evaluating, and improving program performance.

This report describes the development and application of the part of the toolkit designed to provide a simple, user-friendly, and high-level summary tool that can describe and compare programs: the RAND Program Classification Tool (R-PCT). It presents documentation of the R-PCT—its rationale, purpose, and uses—as well as the tool itself, which consists of a set of questions and responses accompanied by detailed guidance for use. The tool was developed through a three-phase iterative process that included a targeted literature review, expert consultation, and preliminary reliability testing to assess the tool's usefulness. Because of its simplicity, the tool is limited to classification (i.e., organizing information for the purposes of describing and comparing) and is not meant for complex analyses or program evaluation.

Although originally developed to support the work of the Defense Centers of Excellence for Psychological Health and Traumatic Brain Injury (DCoE), the R-PCT has broad applicability to many types of programs that support service members and the general public. The contents of this report will be of particular interest to national policymakers within DoD and should also be useful for health policy officials within the U.S. Department of Veterans Affairs (VA), as well as policymakers in other sectors who sponsor or manage programs to support psychological health more generally. The R-PCT is also available at the "Innovative Practices for Psychological Health and Traumatic Brain Injury" web page;[1] other tools in this series will be available at this link as they are prepared.

This research was sponsored by the Office of the Secretary of Defense and the Defense Centers of Excellence for Psychological Health and Traumatic Brain Injury and conducted within the Forces and Resources Policy Center of the RAND National Defense Research Institute, a federally funded research and development center sponsored by the Office of the Secretary of Defense, the Joint Staff, the Unified Combatant Commands, the Navy, the Marine Corps, the defense agencies, and the defense Intelligence Community.

---

[1] http://www.rand.org/multi/military/innovative-practices.html

For more information on the RAND Forces and Resources Policy Center, see http://www.rand.org/nsrd/ndri/centers/frp.html or contact the director (contact information is provided on the web page).

Contents

Preface iii

Figures and Tables vii

Summary ix

Acknowledgments xiii

Abbreviations xv

CHAPTER ONE

Introduction 1
Background 1
Motivation for a Tool to Describe and Classify Programs 2
Purpose of the RAND Program Classification Tool 2
Organization of This Report 3

CHAPTER TWO

Development of the RAND Program Classification Tool 5
What Is a Program and What Are the Defining Characteristics of Programs? 5
    Defining a "Program" 6
    Identifying Characteristics of a Program 7
Creation of a Simple Tool to Describe and Compare DoD Programs Targeting
    Psychological Health and Traumatic Brain Injury 8
    Initial Pilot Testing of R-PCT Questions and Response Options 9
    Testing Inter-Rater Reliability of R-PCT Questions and Response Options 10

CHAPTER THREE

User's Guide for Applying the RAND Program Classification Tool 13
How to Apply the R-PCT 17
Coding Responses to R-PCT Questions 17
Adapting or Updating the R-PCT to Your Portfolio of Programs 32

CHAPTER FOUR

Potential Uses of the RAND Program Classification Tool 35
Example One: Describe Program Barriers Across All Programs 35
Example Two: Describe the Status of Evaluation Activities Across All Programs 36
Example Three: Describe Changes in Programs over Time 36
Example Four: Compare Programs Across Two R-PCT Characteristics 37

Example Five: Compare Programs Using Three or More Characteristics.............................. 38
Example Six: Use as a Diagnostic Tool... 38

CHAPTER FIVE
Conclusions and Next Steps 39
Recommended Next Steps... 40
    Expand the R-PCT to Describe Programs Along a Continuum Based on Their
        Structure and Intensity... 40
    Tailor the R-PCT to a Different User's Portfolio of Programs or a Different Content Area........ 41

APPENDIXES
A. Sources Used in RAND Program Classification Tool Development 43
B. Definitions of a "Program"...47
C. Inter-Rater Reliability Statistics for the Application of the RAND Program
    Classification Tool... 49
D. Training External Raters to Use the RAND Program Classification Tool.................... 51
E. Glossary..53

References 55

Figures and Tables

Figures

5.1   Plot of Programs Placed Along a Continuum According to Structure and Intensity......41
5.2   Plot of Programs Placed Along a Continuum That Could Help Categorize Programs .. 42

Tables

2.1   Guiding Questions and Corresponding Tool Development Activity 5
2.2   Core Program Characteristics.. 8
2.3   R-PCT Characteristics and Rationale for Their Inclusion................................. 10
3.1   RAND Program Classification Tool 13
3.2   Questions for External Raters to Share with Program Staff Before R-PCT Interview 17
3.3   Adapting Response Options for the Scale Question to School-Based Programs........... 32
3.4   Checklist for Adapting the R-PCT to a New Program Portfolio 33
4.1   Cross-Tabulation of Responses to Two R-PCT Outcome Evaluation Questions 36
4.2   Fictional Program's Response to Two R-PCT Characteristics over Time.................. 37
4.3   Cross-Tabulation of Scale and Transferability... 37
4.4   Cross-Tabulation of Scale, Transferability, and Participant Interaction.................. 38

Summary

Despite the recent drawdown of troops in Iraq, the increased pace of deployments over the past decade, longer deployments, and frequent redeployments have resulted in significant mental health problems among service members. Among those who had been deployed to Iraq and Afghanistan as of October 2007, approximately one-fifth reported symptoms consistent with current posttraumatic stress disorder (PTSD) or major depression, and about the same number reported having experienced a probable TBI while deployed (Tanielian and Jaycox, 2008). In the wake of the 2007 report of the DoD Task Force on Mental Health (Department of Defense Task Force on Mental Health, 2007), DoD has implemented numerous programs, interventions, and policies to address the increased prevalence of these conditions and their effects on service members and their families.

As these efforts have proliferated, it has become more challenging for DoD to monitor these programs and to avoid potential duplication of effort. To support DoD efforts in this area, RAND compiled a comprehensive catalog of relevant programs and created a taxonomy for them (see Weinick et al., 2011). In developing the catalog of DoD programs related to psychological health and TBI, RAND encountered a fundamental problem: the lack of a single, clear, universally accepted definition of the term *program*.

To help in creating the catalog, RAND developed a conceptual framework that distinguishes programs from other types of services that may be used by service members and their families. While this framework distinguishes programs from routine services and systems of care, it does not provide operational guidance about how to bound the set of activities that constitute a program or how to identify variation among programs. The lack of an operational definition of a program creates some practical challenges for individuals who manage portfolios of programs.

To address this gap, we developed the RAND Program Classification Tool (R-PCT) to allow users to understand and compare programs, particularly those related to psychological health and TBI, along key dimensions. The tool consists of a set of questions and responses for consistently describing various aspects of programs, along with detailed guidance regarding how to select the appropriate responses. This report describes how the R-PCT was developed and explains how the tool can be used.

The R-PCT is one tool created as part of a larger effort to catalog and evaluate programs related to psychological health and TBI. Information on this and other tools is available at the "Innovative Practices for Psychological Health and Traumatic Brain Injury" web page.[1]

---

[1]   http://www.rand.org/multi/military/innovative-practices.html

How the R-PCT Was Developed

We first conducted a literature review to identify how the term *program* is defined across various fields of study and to identify defining characteristics of programs. After this review, we consulted a variety of experts, including those based at DCoE, regarding which characteristics are of greatest importance in the context of military mental health, and then used this feedback to help focus the review findings into eight essential program characteristics:

- Program goals
- Program barriers
- Evaluation experience
- Evaluation readiness
- Participant interaction
- Scale
- Scope
- Transferability

We then developed a specific set of questions corresponding to these key characteristics to enable descriptions of DoD-funded psychological health and TBI programs.

Once the characteristics and questions were finalized, we developed corresponding response options that would target responses to the questions for each of the specified characteristics and make scoring simple and consistent when the R-PCT was applied by different individuals and to different programs. To develop both relevant questions and response options, we examined the existing literature in the field of program evaluation. We subsequently engaged RAND researchers in a pilot test of the R-PCT to assess how well the characteristics, questions, and response options captured the variability in programs as well as their usefulness for comparing multiple programs.

Characteristics and Questions Included in the R-PCT

The R-PCT includes eight characteristics for describing and characterizing programs. Table 2.3 shows each of these characteristics, along with the rationale for their inclusion. The complete tool, with questions and response options addressing each characteristic, is on pages 13–16 of the report, along with a brief user's guide (Chapter 3) with instructions for how to answer each question, and examples of how to code responses. When applied to a portfolio of programs, the R-PCT could be used to describe and compare a wide variety of programs.

Suggested Uses of the R-PCT

Individuals who manage portfolios of programs (e.g., those who work for government agencies, foundations, and intermediary and grant-making organizations) could use the R-PCT to describe and compare the programs they manage. For example, examining the frequency of responses to the question on program barriers could be a way to identify common barriers faced by multiple programs. R-PCT information about program evaluations (e.g., whether a program has conducted an outcome evaluation in the past year) can provide useful data about the extent to which programs within a portfolio are being evaluated. If used more than once during a program's implementation, the R-PCT would allow users to describe changes in program characteristics over time. If a program portfolio manager is trying to compare programs to identify the best candidates for scaling up, he may want to use R-PCT data on the transferability and scale of current programs. Finally, if a program manager is trying to decide whether a new program should be developed or funded, she may want to use the R-PCT to help identify whether the goals of the new program fill a gap in their portfolio.

Conclusions

The R-PCT is an instrument containing questions and response options across eight core domains that allows managers of a portfolio of programs to quickly, easily, and consistently describe and compare their programs. The program characteristics included in the R-PCT are integral to understanding the goals and objectives of programs and how they function, and offer a set of characteristics along which programs may be delineated. Having consistent metrics is crucial for enabling comparisons of the characteristics of multiple programs in the same content area, and is a first step to developing a more robust operational definition of a program.

The tool (a short set of questions and response options) is not meant to replace more formal program evaluation efforts but to provide a simple, user-friendly way to systematically aggregate data across multiple programs so that individuals managing multiple programs can quickly and easily describe and compare the programs in their portfolio. This information can also inform decisions about what types of technical assistance (e.g., help designing or implementing an outcome evaluation) are needed and for which programs.

We recommend that users continue to adapt and expand the R-PCT, with the ultimate goal of using the R-PCT to classify programs into a typology, which would allow users to better target technical assistance to specific types of programs. In addition to enhancing the R-PCT itself, we also recommend that the R-PCT continue to be tailored for use across a variety of program types. Although developed for use in understanding psychological health and TBI programs, the R-PCT is not specific to a single content area and can be used, with modification, to describe characteristics of programs across a variety of subject areas.

Acknowledgments

We gratefully acknowledge the assistance of the researchers on the RAND Innovative Practices in Psychological Health team who contributed to the development and testing of the RAND Program Classification Tool: Ellen Beckjord, Laurie Martin, Michael Fisher, Todd Helmus, Lisa Jaycox, Kerry Reynolds, and Deborah Scharf. We also thank our project monitors at the Defense Centers of Excellence for Psychological Health and Traumatic Brain Injury, Col Christopher Robinson and CAPT Edward Simmer, as well as Dr. Wendy Tenhula, for their support of our work. We also thank Matthew Chinman, Chris Coryn, and Sarah Hunter for reviewing earlier versions of this report.

Abbreviations

DCoE	Defense Centers of Excellence for Psychological Health and Traumatic Brain Injury
DoD	U.S. Department of Defense
PTSD	posttraumatic stress disorder
R-PCT	RAND Program Classification Tool
TBI	traumatic brain injury

CHAPTER ONE

Introduction

Background

Between 2001 and late 2010, more than 2.2 million service members were deployed in support of military operations in Iraq and Afghanistan, including Operation Iraqi Freedom, Operation Enduring Freedom, and the newest phase of operations in Iraq, Operation New Dawn (U.S. Department of Veterans Affairs Office of Public Health and Environmental Hazards, 2010). Despite the recent drawdown of troops in Iraq, service members have experienced significant mental health problems because of the increased pace of deployments, longer deployments, and frequent redeployments over the past decade. Among those who had been deployed to Iraq and Afghanistan as of October 2007, approximately one-fifth reported symptoms consistent with current posttraumatic stress disorder (PTSD) or major depression, and about the same number reported having experienced a probable traumatic brain injury (TBI) while deployed (Tanielian and Jaycox, 2008). The psychological health of returning service members may also have consequences for their families, as struggles related to PTSD, depression, or TBI may affect marriage and intimate relationships, the well-being of spouses and partners, parenting practices, and children's outcomes (Tanielian, Jaycox, 2008; Chandra et al., 2010).

In the wake of the 2007 report of the Department of Defense (DoD) Task Force on Mental Health (Department of Defense Task Force on Mental Health, 2007), DoD has implemented numerous programs to address the increased prevalence of these conditions and their effects on service members and their families. These efforts aim to reduce the incidence of mental health problems by improving readiness and resilience; providing information, connecting individuals to care, and encouraging help seeking; increasing early identification of individuals with mental health concerns or TBI; providing or improving clinical services, or offering mental health services in nontraditional locations to expand access to care; providing a wide range of training and educational activities; or supporting service members and their families during times of military transition (Weinick et al., 2011).

As these efforts have proliferated, it has become more challenging for DoD to monitor progress and avoid potential duplication of effort. To support DoD efforts in this area, RAND compiled a comprehensive catalog of relevant psychological health and TBI programs and created a taxonomy for classifying such programs. Between December 2009 and August 2010, RAND researchers conducted interviews with program officials to collect detailed information on each program's mission and goals, targeted populations, services and activities provided, outreach strategies, program size, barriers to program participation, funding sources and amounts, and evaluation efforts to date. The catalog and a description of its development are available in Weinick et al. (2011).

Motivation for a Tool to Describe and Classify Programs

In developing this catalog, RAND researchers faced a fundamental challenge: There was no single, clear, universally accepted operational definition of what constituted a *program*. In many instances, even the literature that specifically focused on guiding program evaluation did not provide a definition of what constitutes a program (e.g., Patton, 2002; Rossi, Lipsey, and Freeman, 2004; Khandeker et al., 2009; Wholey et al., 2010). Without a clear definition, it would be difficult to ascertain which initiatives or efforts to include in the catalog or how to systematically describe and organize those initiatives. To support RAND's work for DoD, the RAND team needed to develop a clearer sense of what defines a program, and therefore undertook two concurrent tasks.

The first task was to decide which activities or initiatives could be considered programs and therefore warranted inclusion in the catalog. To that end, RAND researchers developed a conceptual framework illustrating the criteria that distinguish programs from other types of activities that may be used by service members and their families. Such programs were included in the catalog, while other types of activities—such as routine clinical services, activities that provide one-way passive transmission of information without an intervention (e.g., suicide prevention hotlines), research projects, and advisory groups—were excluded. More detailed information about the framework is provided in Weinick et al. (2011).

The second task was the development of a process or tool that would allow RAND researchers to consistently describe and compare multiple programs according to a set of core program characteristics. While the framework in Weinick et al. (2011) provided guidance about what the catalog would include, those efforts did not address the larger challenge—the absence of an operational definition of a program. An operational definition that identifies the concrete operations or processes that constitute a program is fundamental to collecting standardized measures across multiple programs.

An important first step to establishing an operational definition of a program is to identify a core set of characteristics that could help characterize programs along key dimensions. Therefore RAND researchers began a task to identify these characteristics and develop a methodology to apply them for the purpose of classifying programs. These efforts resulted in the RAND Program Classification Tool (R-PCT), which consists of a set of questions and responses that enable users to consistently describe components and attributes of programs of interest. We selected the term *classification* because it connotes the aim of the tool—to organize information using a simple framework so that multiple programs can be described and compared quickly and easily. Although the R-PCT provides only a limited operational definition of a program, it does identify core program characteristics that with further effort could be used to inform such an operational definition.

Purpose of the RAND Program Classification Tool

The R-PCT provides a simple, user-friendly and high-level tool that can quickly and easily aggregate data from multiple programs to better describe and compare them. The tool offers a set of dimensions that are integral to understanding how programs function and by which programs may be consistently characterized. Since programs can offer a variety of activities, depending on the program's goals or mission, the purpose of the R-PCT is not to present a definitive answer as to whether an initiative or effort is or is not a program, but to offer a set of characteristics that can be used to describe or compare a program.

Although the tool was developed specifically to describe and compare programs focused on psychological health and TBI within a military context, its components are broad enough so that users can apply the tool to describe characteristics of programs across a variety of subject areas and in other sectors. For example, the tool enables users to look across a portfolio of multiple programs to compare goals, evaluation activities, or barriers, or to help inform decisions about additional training or technical assistance needed by program staff. The R-PCT could therefore support further efforts in cataloging DoD programs and/or be used to describe new or emerging programs across a variety of subject areas and organizations.

The R-PCT is designed to be easy to use and accessible to individuals who do not have expertise in program evaluation. However, there are some limitations to the tool. For example, it is beyond the scope of the tool to assist users in evaluating programs' progress in meeting their stated goals. It is not meant to replace an Evaluability Assessment (in which one ascertains how feasible an evaluation is), development of a logic model (in which linkages between goals, outcomes, and activities are explicitly illustrated), or monitoring the implementation of program features. Important to note is that the R-PCT is not intended to take the place of a rigorous program evaluation. Furthermore, in order for the tool to be most useful to a variety of potential users, validation is required to ensure that the tool's key domains, questions, and response categories best characterize programs in a specific content area.

The R-PCT is part of a larger toolkit being developed by RAND to catalog and evaluate programs related to psychological health and TBI. Information on this and other tools is available at http://militaryhealth.rand.org/innovative-practices.

Organization of This Report

This report presents the R-PCT to potential users, describes the process by which RAND developed the R-PCT, provides guidance on how to apply the tool, and suggests possible uses of the tool to meet the needs of users. It is organized according to three guiding questions:

1. What is a program and what are the defining characteristics of programs?
2. How can these characteristics be used to create a simple tool to describe and compare DoD programs targeting psychological health and TBI?
3. How can DoD and other stakeholders with an interest in describing and comparing programs use this tool?

Chapter Two describes the literature review and expert consultation used to define what a program is, identify the defining characteristics of a program, and develop the questions used in the R-PCT. Chapter Three presents the R-PCT and applies the R-PCT to an example program, offering guidance on how to respond to the questions posed in the tool and how users should code these responses. Chapter Four describes potential uses of the R-PCT. Chapter Five provides concluding thoughts and next steps. Appendix A lists sources that were used in the literature review described in Chapter Two. Appendix B lists the definitions of a program identified during the targeted literature review. Appendix C reports the results of our analyses of the inter-rater reliability of the R-PCT. Appendix D describes how to train external raters to use the R-PCT and provides a sample training agenda. Appendix E contains a glossary of relevant terms.

Development of the RAND Program Classification Tool

The R-PCT was developed concurrently with RAND's catalog of psychological health and TBI programs and the development of criteria for including programs in the catalog. As such, the development process was iterative and fluid.

The development process consisted of three activities: (1) a targeted literature review; (2) consultation with experts in the fields of program evaluation, psychological health, social services, and military health; and (3) preliminary reliability testing to assess the tool's usefulness. For each activity, we constructed and then revised the tool in response to comments and critiques from experts. Table 2.1 itemizes the methods used to answer each of the three questions that guided the tool's development. In the remainder of this section, we describe each step of the tool development process.

What Is a Program and What Are the Defining Characteristics of Programs?

We first conducted a targeted literature review of the publications in military studies, public health, and psychological health to capture the key characteristics used to define, bound, and conceptualize a *program*. This literature review was not meant to be exhaustive or to serve as a meta-analysis, but narrowly focused on answering a set of guiding questions. The purpose was to develop an understanding of the range of ways in which each field defines and characterizes programs. A list of sources used in the review, organized by subject area, is available in Appendix A.

Table 2.1
Guiding Questions and Corresponding Tool Development Activity

Guiding Question	Tool Development Activity
What is a program and what are the defining characteristics of programs?	• Targeted literature review
How can these characteristics be used to create a simple tool to describe and compare DoD programs?	• Expert consultation • Preliminary reliability testing
How can DoD and other stakeholders with an interest in describing and comparing programs use this tool?	• Expert consultation • Development of user's guide

Three questions guided the literature review:

1.   How is *program* defined in the literature from each of these fields?
2.   What are the common elements in how a program is defined across these fields?
3.   What are the common characteristics considered by each field when comparing multiple programs?

We conducted a keyword search of the online databases PubMed and PsycINFO, and the journal *Military Psychology*, using the search terms *program* AND *definition* OR *framework* OR *typology*. The search yielded 1,124 potential articles. We also asked experts to suggest key documents pertinent to this subject area. Experts submitted six documents for consideration. Two of the authors conducted a title and abstract review of all of these documents, narrowing the list to 21 journal articles and 18 books, for a total of 39 peer-reviewed documents. Documents were included if they provided a conceptual or theoretical description of the key characteristics that define or constitute a program. We specifically looked for studies that advanced the conceptual and theoretical definition and description of programs, such as frameworks and typologies. Literature was excluded from the review if it focused solely on an evaluation of a single program, was not available in English, or focused on computer programming. We did not review a large number of evaluation studies to determine what the common elements of a program were because this level of review was beyond the scope of the current effort. However, future studies may wish to use such an approach to broaden the results reported here.

A data abstraction form was used by two of the authors to ensure that consistent information was abstracted from the 39 peer-reviewed documents listed in Appendix A. The abstraction form captured the reference documentation, any definitions of the term *program*, and any characteristics used to describe or compare programs. The authors each abstracted information from three documents, and then discussed how they used the data abstraction form (i.e., the rationale behind each piece of information extracted). This discussion resolved any discrepancies in how they were using the form and served to improve the consistency of future abstraction efforts. Once the abstraction of information was complete, the authors synthesized the abstracted data into a list of definitions and core characteristics of programs that were common across fields, could be used to describe programs in a consistent manner, and should therefore be considered for the tool.

Defining a "Program"

During the targeted literature review, we identified eight different definitions of the term *program* (see Appendix B). It is noteworthy that of the 39 documents reviewed, only nine included a definition of the term *program*. The definitions were primarily found in federal government documents and textbooks. These eight definitions were synthesized by the authors to identify the common elements that are included in our limited operational definition of a program: A set of activities, tied together through shared resources (e.g., staff, funding, space, materials), meant to impact a targeted population's knowledge, attitudes, and/or behavior in order to accomplish a specific goal or goals.

This definition, as well as the array of definitions we identified in the literature (reported in Appendix B), provide simple guidance about what constitutes a program but are limited in two key ways. First, applying the definition to a group of efforts would capture all types of efforts—from a set of loosely coupled activities to more structured efforts—regardless of whether they are externally or internally labeled or identified as a program. While grouping all types of efforts together as programs can provide useful information about the array of activities being conducted by DoD, the lack of distinction among efforts may also create some practical challenges (Khandeker et al., 2009). For example, portfolio managers trying to select programs that may be good candidates for replication may want to narrow down the list of programs to only those that are very specifically defined.

Second, a brief definition like this does not provide any guidance about how to bound the set of activities that compose a program. Program evaluators have found that in many cases there is disagreement about what resources or activities are considered part of a program (Wholey et al., 2010). The development of a logic model is one strategy that has been used to identify the theory or rationale behind a program and provide some boundaries on what is considered part of a program's structure (Riemer and Bickman, 2011; Wholey et al., 2010). A logic model is an illustrative diagram that outlines a theory of how a program's services or activities result in short- or long-term impacts (Knowlton and Phillips, 2009; such an outline is also referred to as a theory of action or theory of impact [Rossi, Lipsey, and Freeman, 2004]).

An Evaluability Assessment is another technique used in the field of program evaluation to determine a program's bounds in the process of gauging a program's readiness for evaluation (Trevisan and Huang, 2003). Developed by Joseph Wholey (Wholey, 1979; Wholey, 1981; Wholey, 1994), an Evaluability Assessment is an exercise to determine whether a program meets the conditions for a meaningful evaluation to take place and whether an evaluation is likely to contribute to improved program performance and management. An Evaluability Assessment can involve a variety of steps, including stakeholder interviews, a review of program documentation, and the review or development of a logic model to understand how a program expects to accomplish its intended outcomes (Leviton et al., 2010). During an Evaluability Assessment, bounds must be placed around the program to make determinations about what the "it" is that is being evaluated.

Although a logic model or an Evaluability Assessment is critical to conducting a program evaluation, the level of effort needed to complete either of these strategies would require significant resources and expertise to collect information across a broad portfolio of programs and may not be necessary if the objective is simply to describe and compare programs. Instead, it may be more helpful to define programs based on just the key characteristics necessary for description or comparison.

Identifying Characteristics of a Program

Findings from the literature review were also used to identify an expanded list of the core characteristics commonly used to describe and compare programs. Identifying such characteristics may allow portfolio managers to quickly and easily obtain a big picture "snapshot" of their portfolio. Core characteristics identified in the literature review captured a program's *structure*, such as whether the initiative had resources, a goal, or participants. Additional characteristics were related to the *quality* of the program, including whether the program is in a position to be evaluated and the extent to which it is transferable to new locations or populations. Other characteristics that were related to the *intensity* of the program included scope, scale, and dosage. See Table 2.2 for the full list of core characteristics.

Table 2.2
Core Program Characteristics

Dimension	Description
A program has a specific structure including	
Goals, objectives, and targeted outcomes	Expected effects (short-term/immediate and long-term) (Praslova, 2010; Fisher et al., 2006; Brousselle and Champagne, 2011; Funnell and Rogers, 2011; Patton, 2002)
Targeted populations	Who the program intends to reach or affect (Brousselle and Champagne, 2011)
Resources	• Human/talent (e.g., staff, volunteers, managers) • Financial/monetary (i.e., budget) • Equipment (i.e., facilities) (Funnell and Rogers, 2011; Slavin, 2008)
Outputs	Products, goods, or services (Coker, Astramovich, and Hoskins, 2006; Zorzi et al., 2002)
Activities	Steps to produce outputs; what the program does to effect change (Durlak and DuPre, 2008; Chen, 1996)
Participants	Individuals receiving services (Wilson and Lipsey, 2007)
A "quality" program is one that is	
Evaluated	Processes are in place to collect data and measure how well the program is meeting its intended goals; program officials use data for decisionmaking, oversight, or monitoring (Lapan, 2001; Stufflebeam and Shinkfield, 2007; McDavid and Hawthorne, 2006; Stake, 2002; Carman, 2007)
Sustained	Processes are in place to support the program's continued existence (Ernst and Hiebert, 2002)
Replicable	Systematized in such a way (e.g., a detailed manual) that suggests transferability, including clear staff roles and responsibilities (Umble, 2007; Chen and Donaldson, 2011)
A program engages its targeted population at the appropriate intensity level in	
Scope	The range of services the program provides (Clark, 1985)
Scale	Size of the program, including geographic area covered (Kellam and Langevin, 2003)
Dosage level	Amount and frequency of services provided (Mertens, 2009)

This list is not meant to be exhaustive, because the definition of the core characteristics of programs are constantly changing (Tyler, 2002), but is meant to serve as the basis for a description and comparison. Next, we show how these characteristics can be used to describe and compare DoD programs addressing psychological health issues and TBI.

Creation of a Simple Tool to Describe and Compare DoD Programs Targeting Psychological Health and Traumatic Brain Injury

We used a three-step process to convert the core program characteristics into an easy-to-use tool, composed of questions and response options to describe and compare DoD programs. First, we tailored the list of characteristics outlined in Table 2.2 to those that were the most relevant to DoD programs. Characteristics were compared against (1) eligibility criteria used to determine which programs would be included in the DoD catalog (Weinick et al., 2011) and (2) information being gathered through informal discussions with DoD program managers. As a result of this cross-comparison, we eliminated three characteristics from the version of the R-PCT used with DoD programs. First, we eliminated *activities* and *outputs* because we determined that categorizing DoD program activities and outputs would duplicate what was being done to compile the catalog (Weinick et al., 2011). Second, we eliminated *sustainability* because the catalog was not collecting information we would have needed to rate programs according to this characteristic. However, if users adapt the R-PCT to other settings, it would be important to include relevant questions about these three characteristics (i.e., programs' activities, outputs, and sustainability).

Second, we developed questions and response options for each characteristic with the help of feedback from 11 experts including clinical psychologists, public policy and public health researchers, and administrators at DCoE. After first drafting questions and response options a priori, we reviewed the data being collected for the catalog (Weinick et al., 2011) to generate response options that captured the variability in existing DoD programs. In addition, eight RAND experts in the fields of program evaluation, military health, and psychological health, as well as RAND researchers who helped compile the catalog, were asked to provide feedback on the identified characteristics, either via telephone conversation or in person. Experts at DCoE were also consulted to understand which domains were of greatest relevance to its needs in the context of military psychological health. During these conversations, we shared the draft list of characteristics and asked experts to (1) identify the characteristics that would be most useful to portfolio managers at DCoE to describe and compare programs, (2) provide feedback on any characteristics that might be missing, and (3) provide feedback on wording for questions and response options to correspond with each characteristic. These informal, iterative discussions further refined the list of core characteristics and assisted in the development of a set of questions for assessing how a given program might be described within this group of more general characteristics.

As a result of these activities, the original list of program characteristics itemized in Table 2.2 was narrowed to eight core characteristics that were included in the R-PCT. These characteristics and the rationale for why each was included are listed in Table 2.3. Although not initially identified through the targeted literature review, experts indicated that a question about program barriers should be included in the R-PCT to allow portfolio managers to conduct a comprehensive scan for common program barriers (Remler, Rachlin, and Glied, 2001; Currie, 2006; Ebenstein and Stange, 2010). Finally, we drafted a document that defined each of these characteristics and provided guidance for answering the questions using the response options (see Chapter Four).

Initial Pilot Testing of R-PCT Questions and Response Options

We tested the usefulness of the tool by applying it to the catalog of programs previously described. We conducted a pilot test of the questions and response options and an assessment of the inter-rater reliability of the R-PCT (see Appendix C). The pilot tests ensured that different individuals using the R-PCT would rate programs in a consistent manner. Pilot testing involved the authors, a single person trained by the developers to apply the R-PCT and gather feedback about the usefulness of the tool and accompanying guidance documents (referred to in this section as the *reviewer*), and the RAND researchers involved in creating the catalog of psychological health for TBI programs sponsored by DoD.

Table 2.3
R-PCT Characteristics and Rationale for Their Inclusion

Characteristic	Rationale for Inclusion
Program goals	Provide direction for the program by describing what the program is trying to accomplish (shorter- and longer-term impacts) and identifying the target population
Program barriers	Impede or discourage the intended target population from participating or receiving services
Evaluation experience	Describes the extent to which program staff are engaged in efforts to assess how effective a program is in reaching its goals
Evaluation readiness	Provides information on the potential for future evaluation, including capacity for data collection or the extent to which program staff have taken steps to collect process or outcome data
Participant interaction	Provides information on the ways in which participants interact with program materials or staff members
Scale	Denotes how widely a program is being implemented or whether the program is being implemented across different settings
Scope	Describes the range of activities a program conducts (e.g., treatment or prevention services) and helps to identify boundaries as to what is and is not part of the program
Transferability	Provides information relevant to program replication, including how well the program is documented (i.e., the extent to which people not currently involved in the program would be able to replicate the services provided and carry out the objectives of the program as designed based on existing documentation) and whether any specific resources are needed for program operation (e.g., specially trained staff, materials needed to conduct activities, and physical space needed such as large meeting halls or small private rooms). Of particular interest for the needs of DoD was whether the program could be transferred for use in theater.

We engaged five of these RAND researchers to apply the R-PCT to 25 randomly selected programs that represented a subset of the programs included in the RAND catalog of psychological health and TBI programs. Each researcher applied the R-PCT to five programs. Researchers were asked to provide feedback on (1) how well the characteristics, questions, and response options that constitute the R-PCT captured the variability in programs, (2) whether questions and response options were clear and interpreted consistently, and (3) how useful the guidance document was for potential users. Another RAND researcher not engaged in developing the R-PCT or applying the R-PCT to programs was asked to act as an independent reviewer and gather the feedback from the five researchers. The reviewer met with each researcher to understand his or her rationale for each response, to receive feedback about the usefulness of the draft guidance document, and to ensure that responses were consistent with the intent of each question and across all of the programs rated by each researcher. After meeting with the five researchers, the reviewer noted the rationale for each researcher's responses and compiled a list of questions that researchers had difficulty answering and why. For areas where the researchers encountered difficulty or responses were inconsistent, the authors and the reviewer worked together to decide upon appropriate changes to the R-PCT and accompanying guidance document, and then developed final versions.

Testing Inter-Rater Reliability of R-PCT Questions and Response Options

After redrafting the R-PCT and guidance document based on the information from the pilot testing, we met with the team of six RAND researchers for a two-hour training session on how to complete the R-PCT and use the guidance document. After discussing the R-PCT questions and guidance document, one program was used as an example for discussion, enabling the authors to identify and resolve any discrepancies in researchers' answers and to address any remaining questions about the R-PCT and the guidance document. After the training, the six RAND researchers were asked to independently complete R-PCT questions for three programs purposefully selected by the authors to represent a range of program types. We compared the researchers' responses across these three programs to assess inter-rater reliability using kappa statistics and percent agreement measures. Overall, there was agreement across this limited sample of researchers and across programs: The overall kappa was 0.62, and the average overall percent agreement measure was 75 percent. Detailed information on the statistics employed to check the inter-rater reliability is available in Appendix C.

CHAPTER THREE

User's Guide for Applying the RAND Program Classification Tool

This chapter focuses on answering the guiding question, "How can DCoE and other stakeholders with an interest in describing and comparing programs make use of this tool?" The final tool includes 16 questions, covering the eight program characteristics described in Chapter Two. Table 3.1, the R-PCT tool, shows each of these characteristics, along with the corresponding questions and response options. The R-PCT in Table 3.1 is tailored to DoD programs addressing psychological health and TBI but can be adapted to describe and compare other programs. This chapter introduces the tool and provides a user's guide to applying the R-PCT with an example program. Directions for using the data generated by the R-PCT are given in Chapter Four. Suggested uses are meant to be explanatory only, and should not be construed as the only potential uses of the R-PCT. The specific responses shown in this chapter, such as references to installations and branches of service, reference DoD programs related to psychological health and TBI, but the R-PCT can be applied to other content areas or organizations.

Table 3.1
RAND Program Classification Tool

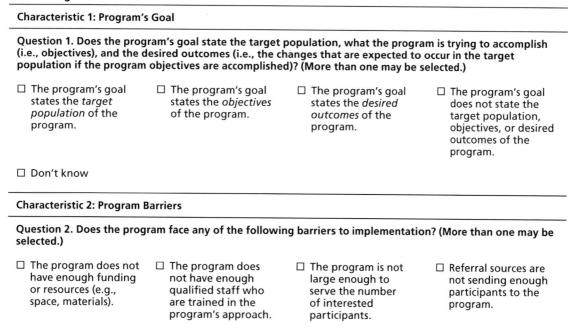

Characteristic 1: Program's Goal

Question 1. Does the program's goal state the target population, what the program is trying to accomplish (i.e., objectives), and the desired outcomes (i.e., the changes that are expected to occur in the target population if the program objectives are accomplished)? (More than one may be selected.)

☐ The program's goal states the *target population* of the program.

☐ The program's goal states the *objectives* of the program.

☐ The program's goal states the *desired outcomes* of the program.

☐ The program's goal does not state the target population, objectives, or desired outcomes of the program.

☐ Don't know

Characteristic 2: Program Barriers

Question 2. Does the program face any of the following barriers to implementation? (More than one may be selected.)

☐ The program does not have enough funding or resources (e.g., space, materials).

☐ The program does not have enough qualified staff who are trained in the program's approach.

☐ The program is not large enough to serve the number of interested participants.

☐ Referral sources are not sending enough participants to the program.

Table 3.1—Continued

☐ Target participants are not aware of the program.	☐ Program staff or service providers are not on board or have not fully bought into the program model (e.g., resistance, lack of participation, or difficulty recruiting staff or providers).	☐ Leadership is not on board (e.g., not ready for the program, does not see the value of the program).	☐ Program logistics are prohibitive to participants (e.g., hours of operation, transportation, space).
☐ Cost of the program is prohibitive to participants.	☐ Adequate time with participants to implement the program is difficult to get.	☐ Perception of stigma is associated with services offered by the program.	☐ Other, please specify:
☐ No known barriers			

Characteristic 3: Evaluation Experience

Question 3.1. Is the program currently collecting any of the following *process* data (focuses on program implementation and operation)? (More than one may be selected.)

☐ Tracking of participation rate or attendance	☐ Tracking of participants (demographic data)	☐ Participant satisfaction surveys	☐ Measures of implementation activities (program fidelity measures such as adherence to the program curriculum)
☐ Other, please specify:	☐ No, not currently collecting any process data	☐ Don't know	

If "No," then ask:
Question 3.2. Has the program ever collected any of the following *process* data (focuses on program implementation and operation)? (More than one may be selected.)

☐ Tracking of participation rate or attendance	☐ Tracking of participants (demographic data)	☐ Participant satisfaction surveys	☐ Measures of implementation activities (fidelity measures such as adherence to program curriculum)
☐ Other, please specify:	☐ No, never collected any process data	☐ Don't know	

Question 3.3. Is the program currently collecting any of the following *outcome* data (used to identify the results of a program's efforts)? (More than one may be selected.)

☐ Pretest/baseline only	☐ Posttest only	☐ Pre-post	☐ Pre-post with comparison group
☐ Randomized controlled trial	☐ Other, please specify:	☐ No, not currently collecting any outcome data	☐ Don't know

If "No," then ask:
Question 3.4. Has the program ever collected any of the following *outcome* data (used to identify the results of a program's efforts)? (More than one may be selected.)

☐ Pretest/baseline only	☐ Posttest only	☐ Pre-post	☐ Pre-post with comparison group
☐ Randomized controlled trial	☐ Other, please specify:	☐ No, never collected any outcome data	☐ Don't know

Table 3.1—Continued

Question 3.5. Has the program conducted an outcome evaluation (assessed whether the program had intended impact) in the past 12 months? (Only one may be selected.)

☐ Yes   ☐ No   ☐ Don't know

Characteristic 4: Evaluation Readiness

Question 4.1. Does the program have goals against which progress could be measured? (Only one may be selected.)

☐ Yes   ☐ No   ☐ Don't know

Question 4.2. Are program activities clearly related to the goals? (Only one may be selected.)

☐ Yes   ☐ No   ☐ Don't know

Question 4.3. How ready is the program for an outcome evaluation? (Only one may be selected.)

☐ The program may be ready now.　☐ The program is probably not ready now, but may be with some clarification or improvements to goals, activities, or procedures.　☐ The program is currently being evaluated.　☐ Evaluation may not be appropriate.

☐ Don't know

Characteristic 5: Participant Interaction

Question 5. Does the program offer standardized services or services that are tailored to each participant's needs? (Only one may be selected.)

☐ The program offers standardized services (same content available or a set number of sessions/ contacts).　☐ Services are tailored based on individual participant needs.　☐ Services are tailored based on group composition or needs.　☐ The program offers both standardized and tailored services.

☐ Don't know

Characteristic 6: Scale

Question 6.1. On what scale is the program being implemented? (Only one may be selected.)

☐ Small scale, being implemented primarily at one installation　☐ Moderate scale, being implemented at more than one installation but not across an entire service　☐ Large scale, being implemented across an entire service　☐ Very large scale, being implemented across multiple services or the entire DoD

☐ Not currently being implemented　☐ Don't know

Question 6.2 What is the anticipated lifespan of the program? (Only one may be selected.)

☐ Short term: less than 1 year　☐ Medium term: 1 to 3 years　☐ Long term: 4 years or longer　☐ No end date: expected to exist in perpetuity

☐ Don't know

Table 3.1—Continued

Characteristic 7: Scope

Question 7. Which activities does the program offer, if any? (More than one may be selected.)

☐ Prevention services

☐ Psychotherapy or counseling

☐ Medical treatment services (e.g., medical tests, surgical care, pharmaceuticals)

☐ Case management services

☐ Assessment/ screening/ referral to appropriate services

☐ Public education

☐ Rehabilitative care (e.g,. physical therapy, occupational therapy, language or verbal communication functioning therapy)

☐ Training for professionals in skills needed to deliver care

☐ Other, please specify:

☐ None

☐ Don't know

Characteristic 8: Transferability

Question 8.1. Does the program require any special resources? (More than one may be selected.)

☐ Technology (e.g., computer, special diagnostic equipment)

☐ Specialized staff (e.g., staff trained in a particular treatment model, child psychologists)

☐ Partnership outside of the military (e.g., outside speaker, outside trainer)

☐ Space (e.g., specific training facility, lab)

☐ None

☐ Other, please specify:

☐ Don't know

Question 8.2. Could the program be implemented in theater? (Only one may be selected.)

☐ No. Program goals and services could not be delivered in theater.

☐ Partially. Some program goals and services could be delivered in theater, but others would need to be adapted, changed, or dropped.

☐ Yes. Program goals and services could be delivered in theater.

☐ Not applicable

☐ Don't know

Question 8.3. Is the program defined and documented adequately to allow it to operate in the same way (with the same target population and in a similar setting) in another location? (Only one may be selected.)

☐ No. The program is not defined well and does not have supporting documentation (e.g., manuals detailing procedures) to be able to operate in another place.

☐ The program would be transferable only if local conditions were the same. The program is well defined and documented, but is customized to the specific location and would require another location to have similar characteristics.

☐ The program would be transferable with more documentation. The program is well defined and could operate in another location if more documentation were created.

☐ Yes. The program documentation clearly describes what the program is and how to operate it (e.g., procedures, required staff/training).

☐ Don't know

How to Apply the R-PCT

In order to ensure that R-PCT questions are answered with little bias, we recommend that an external rater complete the R-PCT after obtaining information about the program from an interview with program staff. If multiple raters will be completing the R-PCT for a set of programs, raters will need to be trained before they apply the R-PCT using techniques to increase inter-rater reliability, such as those described in Chapter Two. Program staff can also complete the R-PCT if they are provided adequate guidance, but self-report may introduce bias and may therefore be less valid than reports from external raters.

The interview with program staff should provide sufficient information so the R-PCT can be completed with confidence. We recommend that the external rater send program staff the open-ended questions listed in Table 3.2 prior to the interview to ensure that program staff are prepared. The external rater can then use the responses to the open-ended questions to complete the R-PCT.

The length of time it takes to complete the R-PCT varies depending on how much information the rater has available about the program; on average, the RAND researchers completed the R-PCT for DoD programs that focus on psychological health for TBI in 15 minutes per program.

Coding Responses to R-PCT Questions

The next section of this chapter explains how to code responses when applying the R-PCT to a single program. The example uses a made-up program referred to as *Fictional Program*. Specifics include the R-PCT questions and response options for each core characteristic, definitions for relevant terms, instructions for application, and sample responses. Since the R-PCT can be used by either an *external rater* conducting an interview with a program official or a *program staff* member completing the R-PCT on his or her own, we provide instructions for both types of respondents on how to obtain answers for each question and code those answers on the response options.

Table 3.2
Questions for External Raters to Share with Program Staff Before R-PCT Interview

- What are the goals and objectives of the program?
- Who is the target population?
- What activities or services constitute the program?
- Does the program face any barriers to successful implementation? If so, what are they?
- Has the program ever conducted a process or outcome evaluation? If so, what type(s) of data did you collect?
- Is the program currently conducting a process or outcome evaluation? If so, what type(s) of data are you collecting?
- How broadly is the program currently being implemented (e.g., across an entire branch of service)?
- What types of documentation accompany the program, such as program manuals, brochures, etc.?
- What types of resources are needed to implement the program?

Characteristic 1: Program's Goal

Question and Response Options

1. Does the program's goal state the target population, what the program is trying to accomplish (i.e., objectives), and the desired outcomes (i.e., the changes that are expected to occur in the target population if the program objectives are accomplished)?

    ☐ The program's goal states the *target population* of the program.

    ☐ The program's goal states the *objectives* of the program.

    ☐ The program's goal states the *desired outcomes* of the program.

    ☐ The program's goal does not state the target population, objectives, or desired outcomes of the program.

    ☐ Don't know

Relevant Terms

*   *Target population* – the participants whom the program is trying to reach
*   *Desired outcomes* – what the program is trying to accomplish
*   *Program objectives* – the means to reach the program's desired outcomes.

How to Answer the Question

External Rater: During the interview with program staff, ask "What is the goal of the program?" As the program staff answer the question, listen for their description of the target population, objectives, and desired outcomes. If program staff provide written material, renew any stated goals verbatim and check with program staff to ensure that the written goal is accurate or adequate.

Program Staff: Review written program materials (e.g., brochure, description, logic model, grant application) to identify a written program goal. Within the written program goal, try to identify a description of the target population, objectives, and desired outcomes.

How to Code the Response

Following are two examples of how the program goals for *Fictional Program* should be scored using the R-PCT.

Example Goal 1.1: *The goal of Fictional Program is to help service members build resilience to stress so they can better cope with the stressors of daily life.*

This goal states the target population (service members) and the desired outcomes (to build resilience to stress so service members can better cope with stressors), but does not indicate program objectives (i.e., what the program is trying to accomplish). Therefore, the external rater or program staff would respond:

☒ The program's goal states the *target population* of the program.

☐ The program's goal states the *objectives* of the program.

☒ The program's goal states the *desired outcomes* of the program.

☐ The program's goal does not state the target population, objectives, or desired outcomes of the program.

☐ Don't know

Example Goal 1.2: *The goal of Fictional Program is to provide training on mindfulness and relaxation to service members in order to build their resilience to stress so they can better cope with the stressors of daily life.*

In addition to the target population and desired outcomes, this goal also states the program objectives (to provide training on mindfulness and relaxation). Therefore, the external rater or program staff would respond:

- ☒ The program's goal states the *target population* of the program.
- ☒ The program's goal states the *objectives* of the program.
- ☒ The program's goal states the *desired outcomes* of the program.
- ☐ The program's goal does not state the target population, objectives, or desired outcomes of the program.
- ☐ Don't know

Characteristic 2: Program Barriers

Question and Response Options

2. Does the program face any of the following barriers to implementation?
    - ☐ The program does not have enough funding or other resources (e.g., space, materials).
    - ☐ The program does not have enough qualified staff who are trained in the program's approach.
    - ☐ The program is not large enough to serve the number of interested participants.
    - ☐ Referral sources are not sending enough participants to the program.
    - ☐ Target participants are not aware of the program.
    - ☐ Program staff or service providers are not on board or have not fully bought into the program model (e.g., resistance, lack of participation, or difficulty recruiting staff or providers).
    - ☐ Leadership is not on board (e.g., not ready for the program, does not see the value of the program).
    - ☐ Program logistics are prohibitive to participants (hours of operation, transportation, space).
    - ☐ Cost of the program is prohibitive to participants.
    - ☐ Adequate time with participants to implement the program is difficult to get.
    - ☐ Perception of stigma is associated with services offered by the program.
    - ☐ Other, please specify:
    - ☐ No known barriers

Relevant Term

- *Program barriers* – challenges preventing optimal program implementation or program success.

How to Answer the Question

External Rater: During the interview with program staff, ask, "Has your program experienced any barriers or challenges to its success, for example with recruiting, implementation, or evaluation?" As the program staff answer the question, make a list of program barriers being described. Once the interview concludes, use this list to code program staff responses using the R-PCT response options. Feel free to code more than one response.

Program Staff: Think about the implementation of the program: Have you experienced any challenges to reaching your goals in terms of recruiting, enrolling, or retaining participants? Have you experienced any challenges to getting buy-in from program staff or the organization housing the program? Have there been any other barriers to fully implementing the program as intended? Finally, if you have an evaluation, have there been any problems getting the evaluation in place, collecting the data you need, or using the data for program improvement? As you are thinking through these questions, check off any of the relevant response options. Feel free to select more than one response.

How to Code the Response

Following is an example of a response to this question and guidance about how to code it.

Example Answer to Question 2: *"We have not had a lot of challenges. I mean, it took us longer to get started than we anticipated because we had <u>trouble getting enough qualified program staff to participate, and are still not fully staffed</u>. And since then, we've not been able to implement all sessions with participants. It has been <u>difficult to find the time for service members to come to the program itself</u> because of all the competing priorities they have. Those are the major challenges we've faced."*

Although the program staff indicated that *Fictional Program* did not face a lot of challenges, there are two challenges stated in the sample response (see the underlined portions). The first challenge underlined would be coded as "☒ The program does not have enough qualified staff who are trained in the program's approach," and the second challenge would be coded as "☒ Adequate time with participants to implement the program is difficult to get."

Characteristic 3: Evaluation Experience

This component has three sections: process data, outcome data, and outcome evaluation.

PROCESS DATA
Questions and Response Options

3.1 Is the program currently collecting any of the following *process* data (focuses on program implementation and operation)?

3.2 If "No," then ask: Has the program ever collected any of the following *process* data (focuses on program implementation and operation)?

☐ Tracking of participation rate or attendance

☐ Tracking of participants (demographic data)

☐ Participant satisfaction surveys

☐ Measures of implementation activities (fidelity measures, such as adherence to the program curriculum)

☐ Other, please specify:

☐ No, not currently collecting any process data / No, never collected any process data

☐ Don't know

Relevant Terms
- *Process or implementation data* – helps a program answer questions about who is being served and whether the program is providing services and activities with fidelity to an original design
- *Evaluation* – a systematic way that data are assembled into a picture of (1) how well an organization is delivering its services (process or implementation evaluation) and (2) the impact of those services on the target population (outcome evaluation).

How to Answer the Questions

External Rater: Ask the program staff whether they have ever collected any process or implementation data. Define the types of data typically used in a process evaluation, such as the number of participants compared to the targeted population over a specified time period (participation rates) or information on the gender, race, or age of people that participate in services (demographic data), to help prompt interview responses. Record responses using the R-PCT. Next, ask the program staff whether they are currently collecting any process or implementation data. Again, record responses using the R-PCT. Feel free to select more than one response.

Program Staff: To prepare to answer this section of the R-PCT, you will need to gather a list of all the data that your program collects, including the date that the program started/stopped collecting each type of data. This may take some time to compile and require reviewing historical documents and/or reaching out to additional program staff. This should be done in advance of answering these questions. Once the list is prepared, cross-reference the list with the response options under Questions 3.1 and 3.2. Feel free to select more than one response.

How to Code the Response

Following is an example of a response to the questions and guidance about how to code it.

Example Answer to Questions 3.1 and 3.2: "*Fictional Program does collect some process data. We want to understand how well we are doing during the classroom portion of the program so <u>we collect some surveys</u> after the classroom portion <u>to see what in-program role modeling activities service members participated in</u> and <u>to understand how happy participants are with our teachers</u>. We also <u>keep track of participant attendance</u>, since service members need to record the hours they spend in the program. I think that's it.*"

The program staff reported collecting three types of process data: (1) record of which activities participants engaged in (implementation activity); (2) assessment of participant satisfaction with teachers or a satisfaction survey; and (3) tracking of attendance. Therefore the response would be:

- ☒ Tracking of participation rate or attendance
- ☐ Tracking of participants (demographic data)
- ☒ Participant satisfaction surveys
- ☒ Measures of implementation activities
- ☐ Other, please specify:
- ☐ No, never collected any process data
- ☐ Don't know

OUTCOME DATA
Questions and Response Options

3.3. Is the program currently collecting any of the following *outcome* data (used to identify the results of a program's efforts)?

3.4. If "No," then ask: Has the program ever collected any of the following *outcome* data (used to identify the results of a program's efforts)?

☐ Pretest/baseline only
☐ Posttest only
☐ Pre-post
☐ Pre-post with comparison group
☐ Randomized controlled trial
☐ Other, please specify:
☐ No, not currently collecting any outcome data / No, has never collected any outcome data
☐ Don't know

Relevant Terms

- *Outcome data* – data that enable the program to measure the *effectiveness* or *impact* of the services provided or whether the program is meeting its intended outcomes; could be collected internally by program officials or by an external organization
- *Pretest/baseline only* – data collected at the beginning of the delivery of any services *before* any services have been provided to or utilized by program participants (no posttest data collected)
- *Posttest only* – data collected only *after* the delivery of services (no pretest/baseline data collected)
- *Pre-post* – data collected both before and after the delivery of services so that the program can compare the two points in time for growth, change, recovery, reintegration, etc. (depending on the goals of the program)
- *Pre-post with comparison group* – typically, comparison of data collected with that of a "control" group that has not received the program services to ascertain whether any changes seen in the target population after receiving program services are different from any changes seen in the comparison group after *not* receiving program services
- *Randomized controlled trial* – considered the "gold standard" of outcome evaluations. Targeted population members are sorted *randomly* into two groups: one that receives the services and another that does not. Data may be collected at multiple time points.

How to Answer the Questions

External Rater: Ask the program staff whether they are currently collecting outcome data on the program (Question 3.3), and record appropriate responses using the previous definitions. Next, if the program staff respond that the program is not currently collecting outcome data, ask whether the program has ever collected any outcome data. For example, if the program staff respond to Question 3.3 that they collected posttest only data, then move on to Question 3.5. In filling out response categories to Question 3.3, you'll likely have to probe about whether the program collects posttest only data from a comparison or control group. Be prepared to ask clarifying questions as needed. If program staff respond that they aren't collecting any outcome data, ask if they ever collected outcome data (Question 3.4), and complete the response categories accordingly.

Program Staff: Using the list you prepared of all the data the program collects, cross-reference the list with the response options under Questions 3.3 and 3.4.

How to Code the Response

Following is an example of a response to the questions and guidance about how to code it.

Example Answer to Questions 3.3 and 3.4: "We do collect some outcomes data from Fictional Program participants. We want to understand whether Fictional Program builds <u>resilience</u> so we are using the Connor-Davidson Resilience Scale and surveying participants <u>before and after</u> the intervention. We're also collecting information on <u>coping styles before and after</u> the intervention. Unfortunately, we have limited resources so are not able to collect data from a comparison or control group. But hopefully, we'll see some changes in outcomes with data we do collect."

The program staff reported collecting outcome data on resilience and coping styles, both before and after the intervention. This would be coded as a "☒ *Pre-post*" under Question 3.3 since data were collected both before and after the delivery of services with the intention to compare the two points in time for growth, change, recovery, reintegration, etc. (depending on the goals of the program).

OUTCOME EVALUATION

Question and Response Options

3.5 Has the program conducted an outcome evaluation (assessed whether the program had intended impact) in the past 12 months?

☐ Yes

☐ No

☐ Don't know

Question 3.5 specifically asks about whether the program has undergone a full outcome evaluation, moving beyond simply collecting outcome data on a routine basis. Such evaluations may be conducted either by program staff or by an external third party.

How to Answer the Question

External Rater: Ask the program staff whether the program has conducted an outcome evaluation in the last 12 months. Select "Yes" if an evaluation has been conducted or if the evaluation is underway, but final results are not yet complete. Select "No" if an evaluation is planned, but has not yet begun. "Don't know" should be used sparingly. When in doubt, ask clarifying questions as needed.

Program Staff: Think about the last 12 months. Has your program conducted an outcome evaluation? This means moving beyond just data collection and using the data you have collected to determine whether your program is having the intended impacts.

How to Code the Response

Following is an example of a response to this question and guidance about how to code it.

Example Answer to Question 3.5: *"Yes, we're currently planning to begin collecting data. We should start in about two months. Then we'll be able to see whether Fictional Program is effective at building resilience among service members."*

Even though the program staff responded "Yes," there is no ongoing program evaluation, and none in the past 12 months. Therefore, this response would be coded as "☒ No."

Characteristic 4: Evaluation Readiness

Questions and Response Options

4.1 Does the program have goals against which progress could be measured?
  ☐ Yes
  ☐ No
  ☐ Don't know

4.2 Are program activities clearly related to the goals?
  ☐ Yes
  ☐ No
  ☐ Don't know

4.3 How ready is the program for an outcome evaluation?
  ☐ The program may be ready now.
  ☐ The program is probably not ready now, but may be with some clarification or improvements in goals, activities, or procedures.
  ☐ The program is currently being evaluated.
  ☐ Evaluation may not be appropriate.
  ☐ Don't know

Relevant Term

• *Goal against which progress could be measured* – a goal that provides an indication of how much change is expected in process or outcome measures and by when.

How to Answer the Questions

External Rater: During this section of the interview, start by asking the program staff, "Do your program goals provide any indication about how much change you expect to see (e.g., 10 percent improvement in coping skills of program participants), or by when this change is expected to occur?" The program staff must be able to describe both a specific amount or magnitude of increase (e.g., a percent change) expected in program participants *and* a date or time period by when the change should occur to score a "☒ Yes" for Question 4.1; if either is unclear, select "☒ No." Next, ask the program staff to describe their program activities and how they relate to their goals. You should specifically probe the goals that were described in response to Question 1 to determine if there are activities assigned to each goal. To select a "☒ Yes" to Question 4.2, the program staff should be able to connect all activities to one or more goals. Question 4.3 is not asked directly of the program staff. Raters should base their response on program staff answers to prior questions (see Scoring Question 4.3).

Program Staff: Think about your program's goals and activities. Do your program's goals identify how much change is expected in participants as a result of participating in your program (e.g., a percent increase) and by when this change is expected (e.g., by the end of the program)? If so, select "☒ Yes" to Question 4.1. If you cannot specify either the amount of change expected or by when the change is expected, select "☒ No." Next, walk through each goal and list the activities connected to the goal. If you can list all your program activities under one or more goals, select "☒ Yes" to Question 4.2; if you cannot, select "☒ No." Your response to Question 4.3 is based on your responses to prior questions (see Scoring Question 4.3).

How to Code the Response

This question is based on answers to previous questions. If you selected "☒ Yes" for Question 3.5 (Has the program conducted an outcome evaluation in the past 12 months?), select "program is currently being evaluated." If you selected "☒ No" to *either* Questions 4.1 or 4.2, the answer to Question 4.3 should be "program is probably not ready now, but may be with some clarification or improvements to goals, activities, or procedures." Marking this response suggests that this program is not currently a good candidate for evaluation, but could be in the near future if members of program staff revisit program goals, activities, *or* procedures. If you selected "☒ No" to *both* Questions 4.1 and 4.2, the answer to 4.3 should be "☒ Evaluation may not be appropriate." Marking this response suggests that this program is not a good candidate for evaluation until program staff revisit goals, activities, *or* procedures.

Following is an example of a response to the questions and guidance about how to code it.

Example Answer to Questions 4.1–4.3: *"Our program specifies that we will see <u>improvements in resilience and coping skills by the end of the program</u>, usually an average of <u>20 percent improvement</u> in skills of participants. That depends on service members' needs when they start the program. But, <u>all our activities are connected to a program goal</u>. We have the eight in-person classes that teach coping skills, which are directly related to the Fictional Program goal to improve service members' ability to cope with stress. In terms of our goal to build resilience, I mean the whole program is dedicated to that. I can't really specify one activity."*

Because Question 3.5 was marked "☒ No," (the program has not conducted an outcome evaluation in the past 12 months) and the program staff members responded that they have a clearly articulated goal (i.e., a 20 percent improvement in resilience and coping skills by the end of the program) and a set of activities related to the goal, the response to Question 4.1 would be coded as "☒ Yes," the response to Question 4.2 would be coded as "☒ Yes," and the response to Question 4.3 would be coded as "☒ Program may be ready now."

Recall that the questions and response options available in the R-PCT allow users to understand the extent to which a process or outcome evaluation has been conducted. This information can then contribute to a R-PCT user's judgment about the readiness of a program for evaluation and can be one part of a larger effort to conduct an Evaluability Assessment. The R-PCT, however, is not designed as a tool for conducting an Evaluability Assessment. More information on Evaluability Assessments can be found in Chapter Two.

Characteristic 5: Participant Interaction

Question and Response Options

5. Does the program offer standardized services or services that are tailored to each participant's needs?
    - ☐ The program offers standardized services (same content available or a set number of sessions/contacts).
    - ☐ Services are tailored based on individual participant needs.
    - ☐ Services are tailored based on group composition or needs.
    - ☐ The program offers both standardized and tailored services.
    - ☐ Don't know

For programs that use a standardized assessment procedure to identify appropriate services for individuals, users should select "☒ The program offers both standardized and tailored services."

Relevant Terms

- *Standardized services* – programs that offer the same content or a set number of sessions/contacts
- *Services tailored based on individual participants' needs* – programs that offer different services to different participants
- *Services are tailored based on group composition or needs* – programs with content tailored specifically to a target population; for example, a program would qualify for this response option if it provides different services for service members in theater than in garrison, or for enlisted service members than officers
- *Program offers both standardized and tailored services* – programs with multiple components, some tailored to participants and some offered to all participants.

How to Answer the Question

External Rater: Ask the program staff to describe the types of activities or services the program provides. Use the response options as prompts, such as asking whether the program offers standardized services or services that are tailored to the needs of individual participants. Select a single response to this question.

Program Staff: Think about the range of activities or services your program offers. Does your program offer standardized services? Or does your program provide services that are tailored to the needs of individual participants or tailored to the needs of a specific group? Select a single response to this question.

How to Code the Response

Following is an example response to this question and guidance about how to code it.

Example Answer to Question 5: *"Fictional Program mostly provides education to service members to teach them mindfulness and relaxation skills. Classes run for six weeks, an hour each week, and we have about 25 participants in each class. Each week we teach a <u>core standardized set of lessons</u>, but we also allow some time for <u>more tailored one-on-one instruction</u> where we help problem solve and provide tips to individual participants."*

Because the program provides both a core set of standardized lessons and tailored one-on-one instruction, the response would be coded as "☒ The program offers both standardized and tailored services."

Characteristic 6: Scale

Questions and Response Options

6.1 On what scale is the program being implemented?
- ☐ Small scale, being implemented primarily at one installation
- ☐ Moderate scale, being implemented at more than one installation but not across an entire service
- ☐ Large scale, being implemented across an entire service
- ☐ Very large scale, being implemented across multiple services or the entire DoD
- ☐ Not currently being implemented
- ☐ Don't know

6.2 What is the anticipated lifespan of the program?
- ☐ Short term: less than 1 year
- ☐ Medium term: 1 to 3 years
- ☐ Long term: 4 years or longer
- ☐ No end date: expected to exist in perpetuity
- ☐ Don't know

How to Answer the Questions

External Rater: Ask the program staff, "How broadly is the program being implemented?" Use the response options as prompts; for example, ask whether the program is being implemented at primarily one installation or across multiple installations. Select a single response to this question. Then ask whether the program has an expected lifespan: "How long is the program supposed to exist?"

Program Staff: Think about how broadly your program is currently being implemented. Is it being implemented across multiple locations or primarily in one location? Select a single response to this question. Next consider whether the program is expected to end at a given time in the future, and choose a single response.

How to Code the Response

Following is an example response to the questions and guidance about how to code it.

Example Answer to Questions 6.1 and 6.2: "We are currently implementing Fictional Program at our Air Force base, but have plans to roll it out across ten more Air Force bases by the end of next year. The Air Force will stick with this program for as long as there is a need."

Although the program staff reported plans to roll the program out across multiple Air Force bases by the end of the year, *Fictional Program* is currently being implemented at only one installation. Therefore, this response should be coded "☒ Small scale, being implemented primarily at one installation." Because the program does not have an anticipated end date, the response to Question 6.2 should be coded "☒ No end date: expected to exist in perpetuity."

Characteristic 7: Scope

Question and Response Options

7. Which activities does the program offer, if any?
   - ☐ Prevention services
   - ☐ Psychotherapy or counseling
   - ☐ Medical treatment services (e.g., medical tests, surgical care, pharmaceuticals)
   - ☐ Case management services
   - ☐ Assessment/screening/referral to appropriate services
   - ☐ Public education
   - ☐ Rehabilitative care (e.g., physical therapy, occupational therapy, language or verbal communication functioning therapy)
   - ☐ Training for professionals in skills needed to deliver care
   - ☐ Other, please specify:
   - ☐ None
   - ☐ Don't know

Relevant Terms

- *Prevention* – services delivered to individuals without a diagnosis to prevent or reduce the likelihood of later problems. These services can target skills such as coping, relaxation, and self-care for mental health professionals.
- *Psychotherapy or counseling* – selected/indicated programs that provide counseling or psychotherapy
- *Medical treatment services* – services delivered by a medical provider or psychiatrist including medical tests, surgery, and pharmaceuticals
- *Case management services* – a collaborative process that assesses, plans, implements, coordinates, monitors, and evaluates the options and services required to meet the client's service needs; can be medical or nonmedical (e.g., refer to offering legal, financial, or educational services)
- *Assessment/screening/referral* – activities to identify a TBI or psychological issue (e.g., offers and scores a depression screening tool online, provides a diagnostic assessment), or specifically refers individuals to care. Providing information about places service members can get help is not the same thing as offering assessment, screening, or referral.
- *Public education* – activities to raise awareness or increase participant's knowledge about psychological health and TBI, and available care options
- *Rehabilitative care* – activities meant to contribute to the physical rehabilitation of service members
- *Training for professionals in skills needed to deliver care* – activities that train professionals on how to deliver treatment effectively.

How to Answer the Question

External Rater: Ask the program staff to describe the activities that constitute their program. As the program staff answer the question, make a list of program activities being described. Once the interview concludes, use this list to code program staff responses using the R-PCT response options. Feel free to code more than one response.

Program Staff: Think about the activities that broadly constitute your program as it is currently being implemented. What is the specific type of service or set of services provided by your program? Choose the correct response from among the response options.

How to Code the Response

Following is an example response to this question and guidance about how to code it.

Example Answer to Question 7: "*Fictional Program provides several services to service members. During times of transition, service members are identified and offered training to help bolster their resilience before deployment. Specifically, service members receive training to ensure they are* educated about positive coping styles to help prevent the development of psychological issues during deployment.*"*

Training of professionals to deliver care should not be confused with training of service members. If training of service members is an activity, users should choose the response option based on the content of training. For example, training of service members that provides psychoeducation about prevalence, signs/symptoms of PTSD, and available resources would be considered a public education activity. In the example answer to Question 7, the training focuses on educating service members about positive coping styles in counseling to *prevent* the development of psychological issues during deployment, which would be coded as "☒ Prevention services."

Characteristic 8: Transferability

Questions and Response Options

  8.1 Does the program require any special resources?
- ☐ Technology (e.g., computer, special diagnostic equipment)
- ☐ Specialized staff (e.g., staff trained in a particular treatment model, child psychologists)
- ☐ Partnership outside of the military (e.g., outside speaker, outside trainer)
- ☐ Space (e.g., specific training facility, lab)
- ☐ Other, please specify:
- ☐ None
- ☐ Don't know

  8.2 Could the program be implemented in theater?
- ☐ No. Program goals and services could not be delivered in theater.
- ☐ Partially. Some program goals and services could be delivered in theater, but others would need to be adapted, changed, or dropped.
- ☐ Yes. Program goals and services could be delivered in theater.
- ☐ Not applicable
- ☐ Don't know

8.3 Is the program defined and documented adequately to allow it to operate in the same way (with the same target population and in a similar setting) in another location?

☐ No. The program is not defined well and does not have supporting documentation (e.g., manuals detailing procedures) to be able to operate in another place.

☐ The program would be transferable only if local conditions were the same. The program is well defined and documented, but is customized to the specific location and would require another location to have similar characteristics.

☐ The program would be transferable with more documentation. The program is well defined and could operate in another location if more documentation were created.

☐ Yes. The program documentation clearly describes what the program is and how to operate it (e.g., procedures, required staff/training).

☐ Don't know

How to Answer the Questions

External Rater: To answer Question 8.1, ask the program staff, "What resources are required to implement the program?" Listen for any of the special resources listed and code all that apply. To answer Question 8.2, ask the program staff, "Is the program being implemented in theater?" See the following scoring instructions for guidance on how to code responses to Question 8.2. To be able to answer Question 8.3, you'll need to ask about whether the program has written documentation such as a training manual or a policy or procedures manual that details information on what program staff should be doing. If staff only have journal articles or a report that briefly describes their program activities, it's likely the program could be transferred but that more information would be needed. Select only one response to Question 8.3.

Program Staff: Make a list of all the resources that are required to implement the program. Use this list to answer Question 8.1, coding any special resources that apply to your program. See the following scoring instructions for guidance on how to code responses to Question 8.2. Next, think about all the written documentation that your program has to support implementation. Does your program have detailed descriptions of program activities documented in a training manual or a policy or procedures manual? Or are only brief written descriptions of program activities available? Using the response options, select a single response to Question 8.3.

How to Code the Response

This question is meant to help identify programs that can be both delivered to and accessed by service members in theater. Select "☒ No" if all of the program activities require staff or other resources that are unavailable in theater. If a program is targeting a specific phase of deployment (e.g., predeployment), it may not be a good fit for providing services in theater. Similarly, if the program requires special resources (Question 8.1) it may not be a good fit for delivery in theater. Select "☒ Partially" if some (but not all) of the program services could be delivered in theater, and "☒ Yes" if *all* the program services could be delivered in theater or if the program is already being implemented in theater. "☒ Don't know" should be selected if you do not have enough information to make a knowledgeable selection. Select "☒ Not applicable" for programs where this question is irrelevant, such as programs that were designed specifically for pre- or postdeployment, or programs for family members. Select only one response to Question 8.2.

Following is an example response to the questions and guidance about how to code it.

Example Answer to Questions 8.1–8.3: *"Our program does have a <u>training manual</u>; it provides guidance on how to train those that deliver the Fictional Program curriculum and provides some <u>general guidance</u> about what should be taught during each class. I mean the same staff are implementing the program regularly, doing the same things while teaching the curriculum but we just have not had the time to write it all down. We are <u>working on a policy and procedures manual</u> that <u>will provide detailed guidance</u> on how to set up, recruit for, implement, and evaluate the program, but that's not quite done yet. The types of resources needed to implement the program are really just the curriculum, teachers—which can really be anyone we train—and a space to hold classes. Nothing special really, although one of the classes requires a psychologist to be present, so you also need a <u>psychologist trained in cognitive behavioral therapy</u> to help with one of the classes. We're really trying to prepare service members for the experiences they will have in theater, so we don't implement the program in theater. Fictional Program is meant to be provided to service members that are getting ready to deploy so we <u>focus on the predeployment period</u>."*

Participants, teachers, and a space with no special requirements are not considered special resources; however, program staff mentioned that a psychologist trained in cognitive behavioral therapy is needed for one class that would be coded as "☒ Specialized staff" under Question 8.1. The program's focus is on predeployment, making it not a good fit for implementation in theater. Therefore, this response to Question 8.2 would be coded as "☒ No. Program goals and services could not be delivered in theater." Finally, the program staff responded that although they have a training manual, it only provides general guidance; more detailed guidance is currently in development but not yet available. Because they have some definition of what they are doing as a program but not enough guidance yet to be transferrable, select "☒ Program would be transferable with more documentation" for Question 8.3.

Adapting or Updating the R-PCT to Your Portfolio of Programs

The R-PCT is designed to be adaptable to any portfolio of programs. The key characteristics and the questions and response options can and should be adapted to the specific contents of a user's portfolio. To adapt the R-PCT, users must assess whether the existing characteristics are appropriate for the programs in their portfolio. First, users should generate a list of descriptions or comparisons of interest. What do you want or need to know about all of the programs in your portfolio? Which characteristics are most important for effective oversight of your programs? What data are you already collecting on your programs, and how could the R-PCT supplement or enhance your knowledge about all the programs in your portfolio?

Next, users will need to review the R-PCT's questions and response options to ensure that they are appropriate for use with a different portfolio and, where necessary, generate questions and response options for any new characteristics. For example, if the R-PCT was being adapted to school-based programs, the response options for the scale question could be adapted from those that are specific to the military community to those that are more appropriate for school-based programs (see Table 3.3).

Once questions and response options are drafted, we suggest that the user rate at least 10 percent of the programs in a portfolio using the R-PCT, making notes where new response options are needed or existing response options are not relevant or need revision. For example, if a portfolio of programs focuses on substance abuse prevention or treatment, the "program barriers" response options may need to be revised to include barriers such as participants' readiness for treatment. After engaging in the rating exercise, final revisions to response options can be made and training of external raters on the new set of response options can begin.

In order to train raters on the final set of questions and response options, users will need to update the user's guide in this chapter. Include updated response options, instructions for how to answer the questions, and an example of how to score a response for each new question. Questions may arise during the initial testing of response options. Record these questions and clarifications as they arise and use them to enhance the user's guide.

Once a final user's guide is drafted, users should distribute the guide and train the external raters. The training should include a review of the guide and an exercise to apply the

Table 3.3
Adapting Response Options for the Scale Question to School-Based Programs

Characteristic 6: Scale
Question 6.1 On what scale is the program being implemented?

Response Options for Programs Serving the Military Community	Response Options for School-Based Programs
Small scale, being implemented primarily at one installation	Small scale, being implemented primarily in a single school
Moderate scale, being implemented at more than one installation but not across an entire service	Moderate scale, being implemented across multiple schools
Large scale, being implemented across an entire service	Large scale, being implemented across an entire school district
Very large scale, being implemented across multiple services or the entire DoD	Very large scale, being implemented across multiple school districts

R-PCT to a subset of programs. Be sure to leave time for review and discussion of ratings so that questions can be clarified and any discrepancies can be resolved. At the end of the training, assess the consistency of R-PCT scores by having multiple individuals apply the R-PCT to the same set of programs drawn from the portfolio. Users may also choose to assess the inter-rater reliability, as described in Appendix C. If R-PCT scores are not consistent (i.e., if inter-rater reliability is low), additional revisions to the R-PCT and supporting materials (e.g., user's guide) and/or additional training may be needed. A description of how to train external raters to use the R-PCT and a sample training agenda is provided in Appendix D. The checklist in Table 3.4 outlines the steps (described previously) that a user will need to adapt the R-PCT for use with a new program portfolio or content area.

Table 3.4
Checklist for Adapting the R-PCT to a New Program Portfolio

1. Have you assessed which program characteristics (from Table 2.2 and Table 2.3) are most relevant to your program portfolio?
   ☐ Yes → Proceed to Item 2.
   ☐ No → Assess which characteristics are missing or need to be revised. The initial list of characteristics may be helpful here (Table 2.2).
2. Do R-PCT questions exist for these program characteristics?
   ☐ Yes → Proceed to Item 3.
   ☐ No → Revise or draft questions according to the list of characteristics identified in response to Item 1.

3. Do R-PCT response options appropriately capture the programs in the portfolio?
   ☐ Yes → Proceed to Item 4.
   ☐ No → Continue testing the R-PCT on programs to enhance response options.

4. Is the user's guide updated to accompany the revised version of R-PCT?
   ☐ Yes → Proceed to Item 5.
   ☐ No → Take this user's guide and update it with additional characteristics, questions, and response options.

5. Have raters been trained on R-PCT questions and response categories using the updated user's guide?
   ☐ Yes → Proceed to Item 6.
   ☐ No → Conduct a training with raters to familiarize them with the tool and accompanying user's guide.

6. Have raters reached a sufficient level of consistency applying the R-PCT? This can be checked through inter-rater reliability.
   ☐ Yes → Move to full application of the tool.
   ☐ No → Retrain raters and redo the inter-rater reliability exercise.

CHAPTER FOUR

Potential Uses of the RAND Program Classification Tool

The R-PCT has a number of potential uses across a wide variety of organizations and activities besides military programs addressing psychological health and TBI. Individuals who manage portfolios of programs (e.g., government agencies, foundations, and intermediary and grant-making organizations) could apply the R-PCT to the programs they manage using the instructions in Chapter Three. Following are examples of how to analyze the data to describe the status of evaluation activities across all programs, to identify common barriers faced by programs, to describe changes in programs over time, and to compare programs across two or more R-PCT characteristics.

Example One: Describe Program Barriers Across All Programs

Looking at even a single R-PCT question can be a useful exercise. For example, looking at the frequency of responses to the R-PCT question on program barriers can identify common barriers faced by multiple programs. When applied to a portfolio of 211 DoD-funded programs focused on psychological health and TBI, the most common barriers to providing services were

- potential participants' concerns about the stigma associated with receiving mental health services (25 percent of programs)
- inadequate funding, resources, or staff capacity to provide services, given the existing demand (22 percent of programs)
- difficulty finding adequate time with program participants (e.g., active duty service members) because of other obligations on their part (18 percent of programs) (Weinick et al., 2011).

Other barriers were mentioned less frequently, including program logistics (such as hours of operation, transportation, and administrative barriers to participation); lack of awareness among potential participants about the program and/or its services; and lack of full support from military leadership. This information was shared with DCoE leadership and could be used to help inform DoD planning of strategies to address barriers to program success.

Example Two: Describe the Status of Evaluation Activities Across All Programs

The R-PCT can be also be used to describe the current evaluation activities of programs. Examining a single evaluation question (e.g., whether a program has conducted an outcome evaluation in the past year) can help determine the extent to which programs are being evaluated. In addition, examining a program using two of the evaluation questions can identify programs that may be candidates for targeted evaluation technical assistance. For example, when applying the R-PCT to DoD-funded or sponsored psychological health and TBI programs, Weinick et al. (2011), found that approximately 23 percent of those programs reported having conducted an outcome evaluation in the past 12 months. In contrast, 45 percent are currently collecting outcome data. This discrepancy suggests that many programs are collecting outcome data that could be used for evaluation purposes, but have not yet initiated or are not currently conducting an outcome evaluation. The R-PCT data from these two questions (as tabulated in the lower left quadrant of Table 4.1) could be used to identify programs that may be candidates for converting their data collection activities into a full outcome evaluation.

Programs that have neither conducted an outcome evaluation in the last 12 months nor are currently collecting any outcome data may require more intensive technical assistance to establish and implement an outcome evaluation plan, as well as resources to begin data collection. Although the R-PCT cannot provide details about specific next steps for technical assistance, it can provide a high-level summary of the current state of evaluation activities to help portfolio managers begin to make decisions about the type and amount of technical assistance they may need.

Example Three: Describe Changes in Programs over Time

If used at more than one time point, the R-PCT also allows users to describe changes in programs over time. In the following example (Table 4.2), a portfolio manager can see that since

Table 4.1
Cross-Tabulation of Responses to Two R-PCT Outcome Evaluation Questions

		Currently Collecting Outcome Data	
		Yes	No
Conducted Outcome Evaluation in Past Year	Yes		
	No	✓	

Table 4.2
Fictional Program's Response to Two R-PCT Characteristics over Time

Fictional Program	Time 1	Time 2
Conducted outcome evaluation in the past year	No	Yes
Program goal states...	The target population and the desired outcomes	What the program is trying to accomplish, the target population, and the desired outcomes

the initial R-PCT responses at Time 1, the program has begun an outcome evaluation and has further clarified their program goal (Time 2).

A portfolio manager can also use the R-PCT to describe changes across an entire port-folio over time. For example, if an organization or foundation decides to invest in technical assistance with the goal of getting more programs in their portfolio to conduct outcome evalu-ations, they could use the R-PCT to examine whether more programs are conducting outcome evaluations *after* the technical assistance than *before* the technical assistance.

Example Four: Compare Programs Across Two R-PCT Characteristics

The R-PCT can also be used to compare one or more programs across two or more R-PCT characteristics. For example, if a program portfolio manager is trying to compare programs to identify the best candidates for broader implementation and dissemination, they may want to use R-PCT data on the transferability and scale of current programs.

For example, programs rated high on transferability that are being implemented on a small scale may be good candidates for larger scale implementation (as highlighted in upper left quadrant of Table 4.3). Although the R-PCT does not provide all the information a port-folio manager would need to make decisions about which programs to scale up (e.g., Is there enough need in the target population?), the R-PCT can be used as one tool to begin identify-ing candidate programs that could be expanded to other populations, locations, installations, or branches of service. For defense-related programs, there is a specific R-PCT question that assesses whether a program could be delivered in theater (i.e., the program is not specific to

Table 4.3
Cross-Tabulation of Scale and Transferability

		Transferability	
		Yes	No
Scale	Small	✓	
	Medium		
	Large		

garrison settings and does not require special resources that are not available in theater), which may be particularly useful for portfolio managers interested in programs to meet growing needs in theater.

Example Five: Compare Programs Using Three or More Characteristics

Similarly, the R-PCT can be used to compare programs based on three or more characteristics. For example, if a portfolio manager has a specific need for (1) a large scale program that (2) may be transferable to other locations and (3) provides services individually tailored to participants' needs, then the R-PCT data could be used to help the portfolio manager identify potential candidate programs. Using R-PCT data on the (1) scale of the program, (2) transferability, and (3) participant interaction, portfolio managers could identify programs with all three needed qualities (as highlighted in lower right-hand quadrant of Table 4.4).

Example Six: Use as a Diagnostic Tool

The R-PCT could also be used by program managers to organize programs that are in the process of being developed or programs that are applying for funding. A program manager could compare the completed R-PCT across all the programs under his or her purview to identify whether the program goals are redundant with existing programs or fill a gap in the existing portfolio of programming. This would enable the program manager to gauge which programs' development or funding should be supported.

Table 4.4
Cross-Tabulation of Scale, Transferability, and Type of Participant Interaction

		Participant Interaction (Blanket vs. Tailored Services)			
		Blanket Services		Tailored to Individual Needs	
		Transferability (Yes/No)			
Scale	Small	No	Yes	No	Yes
	Medium	No	Yes	No	Yes
	Large	No	Yes	No	Yes

CHAPTER FIVE
Conclusions and Next Steps

Consistent metrics are necessary to enable comparisons of the characteristics of multiple programs in the same content area. The R-PCT supports such comparisons by defining the key characteristics of programs, providing questions and response options for gathering information, and allowing users to systematically aggregate data on multiple programs.

Although the tool was initially developed for use by RAND as part of an independent assessment of DoD-funded psychological health and TBI programs, it has broader applicability to describing and characterizing programs that provide other types of services in other content areas, including

- development of program goals (target populations, program objectives, and understanding the expected changes in the target population if the objectives are achieved)
- evaluation readiness (whether the programs have evaluation activities in place, or the extent to which they are prepared for such activities)
- transferability (the extent to which programs have written documentation of policies and procedures to enable implementation in other settings)
- common barriers that programs may encounter.

The strengths of the R-PCT are that it is simple, user friendly, and quick to administer, and provides a high-level description, comparison, or classification of programs. Furthermore, given its simple architecture, the R-PCT can be readily adapted and tailored to meet the needs of potential users. The questions and response options of the R-PCT presented in this report can be expanded or changed so that they ask all potentially relevant questions which portfolio managers need to make decisions.

Prior to wide application and as part of the adaptation process, potential users will need to revisit the methods employed to develop the R-PCT provided in this report. First, the R-PCT in Chapter Three only reflects those characteristics identified in the targeted literature review and through consultation with subject matter experts. Second, aside from the calibration process, the development of the R-PCT did not contain any additional validation activities. Because the inter-rater reliability testing was limited to a sample of six researchers trained to use the R-PCT, users should consider additional reliability testing to assess whether the R-PCT can be used consistently among external raters or program staff using the tool. We suggest several next steps to expand and enhance the R-PCT for further use.

Recommended Next Steps

Expand the R-PCT to Describe Programs Along a Continuum Based on Their Structure and Intensity

To assist in organizing a portfolio of programs, users could answer a set of questions that ask respondents to summarize the information from the original R-PCT questions to gauge how structured a program is (the extent to which the program has defined and standardized policies and procedures) and the level of intensity of the program (the amount of intervention delivered by the program to users). Answers to questions on goals, barriers, data collection and evaluation experience, evaluation readiness, and transferability could help ascertain how structured a program is; and answers to questions on scope, scale, and participant interaction could help ascertain the intensity of engagement of the program.

If the R-PCT were to be further developed, we recommend establishing and testing fuller scales for many of the R-PCT characteristics. For example, programs could be assessed on a six-point scale, such as:

Overall, how structured is the program?

1	2	3	4	5	6
Very unstructured	Unstructured	Somewhat unstructured	Somewhat structured	Structured	Very structured

Overall, how intense is the program?

1	2	3	4	5	6
Very low intensity	Low intensity	Somewhat low intensity	Somewhat high intensity	High intensity	Very high intensity

Users could then plot each program's structure and intensity scores onto a chart with four quadrants, as illustrated in Figure 5.1, which includes example programs (Programs A, B, C, and D) to show where they would be classified on the graph. For example, programs that are high intensity and occur more frequently and over longer time periods (e.g., six months or a year) would fall in the upper and lower right quadrants of the chart (Programs B and D), and programs that are very structured would fall into the upper quadrants of the chart on either the left or the right (Programs A and B).

Expanding the R-PCT to capture structure and intensity (such as by using the six-point scales previously described) could enhance the utility of the tool and help further classify programs into specific categories. These specific categories could be used to create a typology of programs with a different type of program represented in each of the 36 cells displayed in Figure 5.2.

Each cell represents a set of similar programs, or a *cluster*, that could be grouped together. Portfolio managers could then use these clusters to better target technical assistance to specific types of programs. For example, technical assistance for programs that are classified as "not very structured" (e.g., Programs G and H in Figure 5.2) may be more focused on establishing measurable goals and objectives, whereas technical assistance for highly structured programs

Figure 5.1
Plot of Programs Placed Along a Continuum According to Structure and Intensity

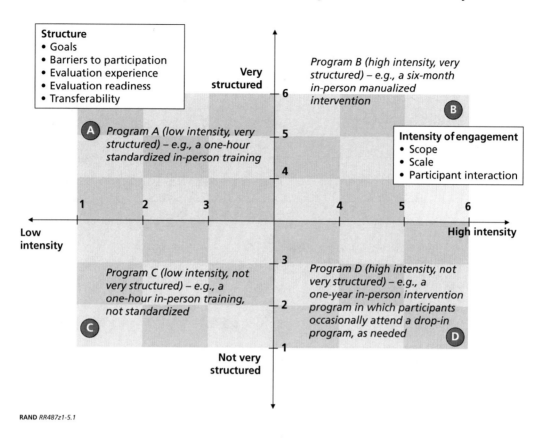

RAND *RR487z1-5.1*

(e.g., Programs E and F in Figure 5.2) may be more focused on identifying relevant measures and troubleshooting data collection issues.

Clusters could also be used to locate similar programs for comparison (i.e., those programs with similar goals for similar target populations). Identifying similar programs may be helpful if program administrators are trying to streamline investments in programs by deduplicating efforts or by having program staff share lessons learned. Program administrators may also wish to reconsider investment in programs that are low in structure and intensity in favor of more highly structured or intense programs if those may be more likely to have an impact on participants. Responses could also be used to refine the structure and intensity scales by providing examples of the types of programs that fall along each continuum.

Tailor the R-PCT to a Different User's Portfolio of Programs or a Different Content Area

In addition to enhancing the R-PCT itself, we also recommend that the R-PCT continue to be tailored for use across a variety of program types. The program characteristics in the R-PCT are integral to understanding the goals and objectives of programs, how they function, and to offering a set of parameters along which programs may be characterized. At the time this report was written, RAND had only applied the R-PCT to programs included as part of a larger study to compile a catalog of psychological health and TBI programs designed to serve members of the military community (Weinick et al., 2011). We would recommend further application of the tool in other content areas.

Figure 5.2
Plot of Programs Placed Along a Continuum That Could Help Categorize Programs

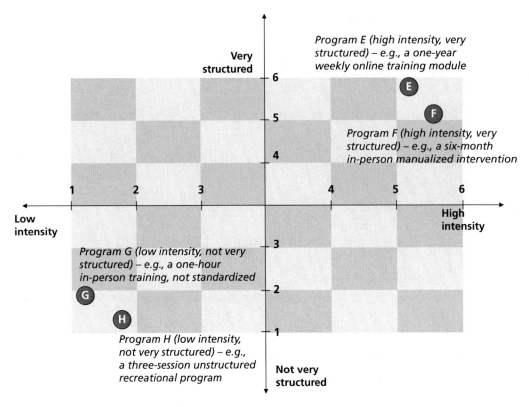

To further adapt the R-PCT to meet users' needs, users should continue to discuss how best to tailor the R-PCT to fit their needs. Some key questions to consider about the R-PCT's application for different users and different content areas:

- Are there other program characteristics relevant to the content area that should be added to the R-PCT?
- Which questions and response options would best enable users to describe, classify, and organize their portfolio of programs?
- How can a portfolio of programs be described beyond a focus on structure and intensity?
- How best can the R-PCT be applied for a given field of study or content area?

We hope that adaptation and application of the R-PCT will continue to stimulate discussion and effort to further operationalize a definition of a program that can be broadly applied.

Sources Used in RAND Program Classification Tool Development

Brousselle A, Champagne F. "Program Theory Evaluation: Logic Analysis." *Evaluation and Program Planning*, 2011, 34 (1): 69–78.

Brownson RC, Baker EA, Left TL, Gillespie KN, et al. *Evidence-Based Public Health.* New York: Oxford University Press, 2010.

Carman JG. "Evaluation Practice Among Community-Based Organizations." *American Journal of Evaluation*, 2007, 28 (1): 60.

Centers for Disease Control and Prevention. "Framework for Program Evaluation in Public Health." *MMWR*, 1999, 48 (RR11): 1–40. As of May 14, 2010:
http://www.cdc.gov/mmwr/preview/mmwrhtml/rr4811a1.htm

Centers for Disease Control and Prevention. Office of the Director, Office of Strategy and Innovation. *Introduction to Program Evaluation for Public Health Programs: A Self-Study Guide.* Atlanta: Centers for Disease Control and Prevention, 2005.

Chen HT. "A Comprehensive Typology for Program Evaluation." *American Journal of Evaluation*, 1996, 17 (2): 121–130.

Chen, HT, Donaldson SI, Mark MM. "Validity Frameworks for Outcome Evaluation." *New Directions for Evaluation*, 2011, 2011 (30): 5–16.

Clark J. "Policy Diffusion and Program Scope." *The Journal of Federalism*, 1985, 15: 61–70.

Coker JK, Astramovich RL, Hoskins WJ. "Introducing the Accountability Bridge Model: A Program Evaluation Framework for School Counselors." In *Vistas: Compelling Perspectives on Counseling 2006.* GR Walz, JC Bleuer, and RK Yep (eds.). Alexandria, VA: American Counseling Association, 2006, pp. 207–210.

Connell JP, Kubiscb AC, Weiss CH, Schorr LB. *New Approaches to Evaluating Community Initiatives. Concepts, Methods, and Contexts. Roundtable on Comprehensive Community Initiatives for Children and Families.* Washington, DC: The Aspen Institute, 1995.

Durlak JA, DuPre EP. "Implementation Matters: A Review of Research on the Influence of Implementation on Program Outcomes and the Factors Affecting Implementation." *American Journal of Community Psychology*, 2008, 41 (3): 327–350.

Ernst K, Hiebert B. "Toward the Development of a Program Evaluation Business Model: Promoting the Longevity of Counselling in Schools." *Canadian Journal of Counselling*, 2002, 36 (1): 73–84.

Fink A. *Evaluation Fundamentals: Insights into the Outcomes, Effectiveness, and Quality of Health Programs.* Thousand Oaks, CA: Sage Publications, 2005.

Fisher D, Imm P, Chinman M, Wandersman A. *Getting to Outcomes with Developmental Assets: Ten Steps to Measuring Success in Youth Programs and Communities.* Minneapolis: Search Institute, 2006.

Funnell SC, Rogers PJ. *Purposeful Program Theory: Effective Use of Theories of Change and Logic Models*, Vol. 31. San Francisco: Jossey-Bass, 2011.

Khandker SR, Koolwal GB, Samad HA. *Handbook on Impact Evaluation: Quantitative Methods and Practices.* Washington, DC: World Bank, 2009.

Knowlton LW, Phillips CC. *The Logic Model Guidebook: Better Strategies for Great Results.* Thousand Oaks, CA: Sage Publications, 2009.

Langbein LI, Felbinger CL. *Public Program Evaluation: A Statistical Guide.* Armonk, NY: Sharpe Reference, 2006.

Lapan RT. "Results-Based Comprehensive Guidance and Counseling Programs: A Framework for Planning and Evaluation." *Professional School Counseling*, 2001, 4 (4): 289–299.

Leviton LC, Khan LK, Rog D, Dawkins N, et al. "Evaluability Assessment to Improve Public Health Policies, Programs, and Practices." *Annual Review of Public Health*, 2010, 31: 213–233.

McDavid JC, Hawthorn LRL. *Program Evaluation & Performance Measurement: An Introduction to Practice.* Thousand Oaks, CA: Sage Publications, 2006.

McLaughlin JA, Jordan GB. "Logic Models: A Tool for Telling Your Program's Performance Story." *Evaluation and Program Planning*, 1999 22 (1): 65–72.

Mertens DM. *Research and Evaluation in Education and Psychology: Integrating Diversity with Quantitative, Qualitative, and Mixed Methods.* Thousand Oaks, CA: Sage Publications, 2009.

Patton M. "Utilization-Focused Evaluation." *Evaluation in Education and Human Services*, 2002, 49 (5): 425–438.

Perepletchikova F, Kazdin AE. "Treatment Integrity and Therapeutic Change: Issues and Research Recommendations." *Clinical Psychology: Science and Practice*, 2005, 12 (4): 365–383.

Poulin ME, Harris PW, Jones PR. "The Significance of Definitions of Success in Program Evaluation." *Evaluation Review*, 2000, 24 (5): 516–536.

Powell RR. "Evaluation Research: An Overview." *Library Trends*, 2006, 55 (1): 102–120.

Praslova L. "Adaptation of Kirkpatrick's Four Level Model of Training Criteria to Assessment of Learning Outcomes and Program Evaluation in Higher Education." *Educational Assessment, Evaluation and Accountability*, 2010, 22 (3): 215–225.

Priest S. "A Program Evaluation Primer." *Journal of Experiential Education*, 2001, 24 (1): 34–40.

Riemer M, Bickman L. "Using Program Theory to Link Social Psychology and Program Evaluation." In *Social Psychology and Evaluation.* M Mark, S Donaldson, B Campbell (eds.). New York: Guilford Press, 2011, pp. 104–140.

Rossi PH, Lipsey MW, Freeman HE. *Evaluation: A Systematic Approach.* Thousand Oaks, CA: Sage Publications, 2004.

Royse D, Thyer BA, Padgett DK. *Program Evaluation: An Introduction.* Belmont, CA: Thomson/Brooks Cole, 2009.

Slavin RE. "Perspectives on Evidence-Based Research in Education: What Works? Issues in Synthesizing Educational Program Evaluations." *Educational Researcher*, 2008, 37 (1): 5–14.

Stake R. "Program Evaluation, Particularly Responsive Evaluation." *Evaluation in Education and Human Services*, 2002, pp. 343–362.

Spaulding DT. *Program Evaluation in Practice: Core Concepts and Examples for Discussion and Analysis.* San Francisco: Jossey-Bass, 2008.

Stufflebeam DL, Shinkfield AJ. *Evaluation Theory, Models, and Applications*, Vol. 3. San Francisco: Jossey-Bass, 2007.

Tyler R. "A Rationale for Program Evaluation," *Evaluation in Education and Human Services*, 2002, pp. 87–96.

Umble KE. "Evaluation for Planning and Improving Leadership Development Programs: A Framework Based on the Baldrige Education Criteria for Performance Excellence." In *The Handbook of Leadership Development Evaluation.* KM Hannum, JW Martineau, C Reinelt (eds.). Hoboken, NJ: John Wiley & Sons, 2007, pp. 464–486.

U.S. Government Accountability Office. *Performance Measurement and Evaluation: Definitions and Relationships.* Publication No. GAO-05-739SP, May 2005. Retrieved from GAO Reports Main Page via GPO Access database. As of October 24, 2011: http://www.gao.gov/special.pubs/gg98026.pdf

Wholey JS, Hatry HP, Newcomer KE. *Handbook of Practical Program Evaluation*, Vol. 19. San Francisco: Jossey-Bass, 2010.

Wilson SJ, Lipsey MW. "School-Based Interventions for Aggressive and Disruptive Behavior: Update of a Meta-Analysis." *American Journal of Preventive Medicine*, 2007, 33: 130–143.

Zorzi R, Perrin B, McGuire M, Long B, et al. "Defining the Benefits, Outputs, and Knowledge Elements of Program Evaluation." *Canadian Journal of Program Evaluation*, 2002, 17 (3): 143–150.

Definitions of a "Program"

Below we list the definitions of a *program* identified during the literature review. The far left column provides the source of the definition, followed by the definition itself. The three columns on the far right represent the three elements that constitute the RAND definition of a program and an "X" indicates that the definition includes the element.

Table B.1

Source	Definition	Set of Activities	Common Goal	Shared Resources
Brownson et al. (2010)	The blending of several interventions within a community.	X		
Centers for Disease Control and Prevention (2005, p. 1)	Any set of organized activities supported by a set of resources to achieve a specific and intended result.	X	X	X
Fink (2005)	A systematic effort to achieve particular planned purposes, such as improvement of health, knowledge, attitudes, behavior, and practice.	X	X	
Langbein and Felbinger (2006)	Ongoing services or activities directed at bringing about collectively shared ends. These ends or goals include the provision of social and other public sector services and the implementation of regulations designed to affect the behavior of individuals, businesses, or organizations.	X	X	
McDavid and Hawthorn (2006)	A group of related activities that is intended to achieve one or several related objectives.	X	X	
Priest (2001)	A collection of several learning experiences held together by logistics such as scheduling, staffing, equipment, meals, housing, transportation, communication, finances, and so on. A learning experience is a specific and individual event in which people engage (directly and indirectly resulting from the program) that subsequently changes the way they feel, think, or behave.	X		X
Royse et al. (2009)	An organized collection of activities to reach certain objectives. Organized activities are a series of planned actions to solve a problem. Interventions or services expected to have some kind of impact on the program participants. Characteristics of a "good program" include staffing, budget, stable funding, their own identity (visible or recognizable by the public), and a core service philosophy.	X	X	X

Table B.1—Continued

Source	Definition	Set of Activities	Common Goal	Shared Resources
Spaulding (2008)	A set of specific activities designed for an intended purpose, with quantifiable goals and objectives	X	X	
U.S. Government Accountability Office (2005, p. 5)	Any activity, project, function, or policy that has an identifiable purpose or set of objectives.		X	

Inter-Rater Reliability Statistics for the Application of the RAND Program Classification Tool

To determine the reliability of responses on the R-PCT, we used several measures of inter-rater reliability, a statistical assessment of the degree of agreement between raters:

- Cohen's kappa (degree of agreement between two raters)
- Fleiss' kappa (degree of agreement among multiple raters)
- Percent agreement (degree of agreement compared to an "ideal rater").

We selected three programs as test cases. Six RAND team members, not including the authors, completed the R-PCT for the three programs. We then calculated the inter-rater reliability of the R-PCT using the above statistics.

First, we used unweighted Cohen's kappa to assess agreement between raters. Cohen's kappa is defined as

$$\kappa = \frac{\Pr(a) - \Pr(e)}{1 - \Pr(e)}$$

where $\Pr(a)$ is the relative observed agreement among two raters and $\Pr(e)$ is the probability of chance agreement. In this way, the Cohen's kappa statistic provides a normalized measure of agreement, adjusted for the agreement expected by chance (Cohen, 1960). Cohen's kappa ranges from –1 to 1, where –1 is complete disagreement, 0 is agreement expected by chance, and 1 is complete agreement. Because Cohen's kappa only allows for comparison between two raters, a matrix was created with the kappas between each combination of raters. inter-rater reliability ranged from 0.40 to 0.79. Each rater's agreement with the other raters was then averaged to provide one statistic per rater. The final kappa scores ranged from 0.56 to 0.69. Kappas within this range are generally considered indicative of agreement (Landis and Koch, 1977).

Second, we used Fleiss' kappa to assess (1) inter-rater reliability for each individual question in the R-PCT, (2) inter-rater reliability for the entire R-PCT, and (3) overall agreement of the raters. Unlike Cohen's kappa, Fleiss' kappa allows for the measurement of agreement among multiple raters. Fleiss' kappa is defined as

$$\kappa = \frac{\overline{P} - \overline{P}_e}{1 - \overline{P}_e}$$

where $1 - \bar{P}_e$ measures the level of agreement attainable beyond what would be expected by chance and $\bar{P} - \bar{P}_e$ measures the actual level of agreement attained beyond chance (Fleiss, 1971). Fleiss' kappa is scaled and interpreted along the same ranges as Cohen's kappa (Fleiss, 1981). The Fleiss' kappa statistics for the individual questions ranged from 0.20 to 1.00. Of the three programs considered, their kappa statistics were 0.79, 0.53, and 0.56. The overall kappa was obtained by giving each program-specific question the same weight and calculating overall agreement. The overall Fleiss' kappa was 0.62, indicating agreement.

Finally, we assessed inter-rater reliability using percent agreement, which allows for a measure of rater agreement that is not adjusted for agreement due to chance. Percent agreement was calculated for each question and subquestion in the R-PCT and then averaged for each of the three programs in the test set. We also calculated an average percent agreement by taking the mean percent agreement for each question, giving equal weight to each question regardless of the number of subquestions in each question. For the three programs in the test set, the average percent agreements were 79 percent, 73 percent, and 74 percent. The average of the overall percent agreement was 75 percent.

These three statistics demonstrate that there was agreement across raters in completing the R-PCT, indicating significant inter-rater reliability and suggesting that, with appropriate training, the R-PCT can be consistently applied to a variety of programs by multiple individuals.

Training External Raters to Use the RAND Program Classification Tool

After adapting the R-PCT and user guide to your portfolio of programs, you will need to train external raters on how to consistently use the R-PCT. Before the training, distribute the updated user guide to external raters so they have time to read though the materials in advance of the training. Begin the training with a review of the updated user guide. Move through each characteristic and review accompanying questions and response options. Questions about how to appropriately use the R-PCT will likely emerge both during and after the training. It is important to establish a process to keep track of questions and your responses so that all external raters remain aware of ongoing decisions. For example, storing the user guide electronically in a shared location (e.g., Google Docs) and highlighting weekly updates would allow external raters to access and review decisions regularly. After reviewing the updated user guide, conduct a calibration exercise with external raters by asking them to rate a sample program using the R-PCT. Then discuss, as a group, what the appropriate ratings should be and resolve any questions or concerns about how to apply the R-PCT. At the end of this group discussion all external raters should be comfortable explaining the rationale behind the sample program's R-PCT ratings.

Next, conduct a more formal inter-rater reliability exercise by asking external raters to review and rate the same three to five programs independently. Compare their responses to determine if they have achieved acceptable inter-rater reliability using the statistics described in Appendix C. If inter-rater reliability is acceptable, external raters are ready to begin implementing the R-PCT. However, if inter-rater reliability is not acceptable, you should hold another group discussion to resolve any differences encountered. After the group discussion, conduct another formal inter-rater reliability exercise. This process should be repeated until your external raters achieve acceptable inter-rater reliability.

A sample training agenda for external raters outlining the aforementioned steps is shown as follows:

Review the Updated User Guide
- Respond to questions
- Discuss process for continued updates to the guide

Calibration Exercise
- Participants review a sample program and rate it using the R-PCT

Group Discussion of Calibration Exercise
- How to resolve differences encountered
- Informal assessment of comfort level with the R-PCT

Inter-Rater Reliability Exercise
- Review and rate three to five programs independently

Glossary

Evaluability Assessment

Investigation undertaken by an evaluator (possibly jointly with evaluation sponsor, program stakeholders, or administrators) to determine whether a program meets the preconditions necessary for evaluation and, if so, how the evaluation should be designed to ensure maximum utility. (Wholey, Hatry, and Newcomer, 2010; Rossi et al., 2004)

fidelity

Adherence of implementation to a program's original design. (Smith, Daunic, and Taylor, 2007)

logic model

A graphic depiction of the rationale and expectations of a program (Leviton et al., 2010). A logic model clarifies the causal relationships among program resources, activities, and outcomes (McLaughlin and Jordan, 1999; Wholey, Hatry, and Newcomer, 2010).

outcomes

Changes or benefits resulting from activities and outputs. Programs typically have short, intermediate, and long-term outcomes. (Leviton et al., 2010; Wholey, Hatry, and Newcomer, 2010)

outcomes evaluation

An assessment of how well the program's activities or services have enacted expected changes in the target population or social condition. (Rossi, Lipsey, and Freeman, 2004)

outputs

The products, goods, and services provided to the program's participants. (Wholey, Hatry, and Newcomer, 2010)

process evaluation

A form of program evaluation designed to document and analyze the early development and actual implementation of a program, assessing whether and how well services are delivered as intended or planned. Also known as implementation assessment. (Wholey, Hatry, and Newcomer, 2010; Rossi, Lipsey, and Freeman, 2004)

program

A set of activities, tied together through shared resources (e.g., staff, funding, space, materials), meant to impact a targeted population's knowledge, attitudes, and/or behavior in order to accomplish specific goal(s). (Chapter Two, Acosta et al., 2012)

theory of change

A model that describes the mechanisms through which the initiative's inputs and activities are thought to lead to desired outcomes. (Leviton et al., 2010)

References

Centers for Disease Control and Prevention. Office of the Director, Office of Strategy and Innovation. *Introduction to Program Evaluation for Public Health Programs: A Self-Study Guide.* Atlanta: Centers for Disease Control and Prevention, 2005.

Chandra A, Lara-Cinosomo S, Jaycox L, Tanielian T, et al. "Children on the Homefront: The Experience of Children From Military Families." *Pediatrics,* 2010, 125 (1): 16–25.

Clark J. "Policy Diffusion and Program Scope." *Journal of Federalism,* 1985, 15: 61–70.

Cohen J. "A Coefficient of Agreement for Nominal Scales." *Educational and Psychological Measurement,* 1960, 20 (1): 37–46.

Currie J. "The Take-Up of Social Benefits." In *Poverty, the Distribution of Income, and Public Policy.* A Auerbach, D Card, and J Quigley (eds.). New York: Russell Sage, 2006, pp. 80–148.

Department of Defense Task Force on Mental Health. *An Achievable Vision: Report of the Department of Defense Task Force on Mental Health.* Falls Church, VA.: Defense Health Board, 2007. As of January 22, 2011: http://www.health.mil/dhb/mhtf/mhtf-report-final.pdf

Ebenstein A, Stange K. "Does Inconvenience Explain Low Take-Up? Evidence from Unemployment Insurance." *Journal of Policy Analysis and Management,* 2010, 29 (1): 111–136.

Fisher D, Imm P, Chinman M, Wandersman A. *Getting to Outcomes with Developmental Assets: Ten Steps to Measuring Success in Youth Programs and Communities.* Minneapolis: Search Institute, 2006.

Fleiss JL. "Measuring Nominal Scale Agreement Among Many Raters." *Psychological Bulletin,* 1971, 76 (5): 378–382.

Fleiss JL. *Statistical Methods for Rates and Proportions,* 2nd ed. New York: John Wiley, 1981, pp. 38–46.

Kellam S, Langevin D. "A Framework for Understanding Evidence in Prevention Research Programs." *Prevention Science,* 2003, 4 (3): 137–153.

Khandker SR, Koolwal GB, Samad HA. *Handbook on Impact Evaluation: Quantitative Methods and Practices.* Washington, DC: World Bank, 2009.

Knowlton LW, Phillips CC. *The Logic Model Guidebook: Better Strategies for Great Results.* Thousand Oaks, CA: Sage Publications, 2009.

Landis JR, Koch GG. "The Measurement of Observer Agreement for Categorical Data." *Biometrics,* 1977, 33: 159–174.

Leviton LC, Khan LK, Rog D, Dawkins N, et al. "Evaluability Assessment to Improve Public Health Policies, Programs, and Practices." *Annual Review of Public Health,* 2010, 31: 213–233.

McLaughlin JA, Jordan GB. "Logic Models: A Tool for Telling Your Program's Performance Story." *Evaluation and Program Planning,* 1999, 22 (1): 65–72.

Patton M. "Utilization-Focused Evaluation." *Evaluation in Education and Human Services,* 2002, 49 (5): 425–438.

Remler DK, Rachlin JE, Glied SA. *What Can the Take-Up of Other Programs Teach Us About How to Improve Take-Up of Health Insurance Programs?* NBER Working Paper No. 8185. Cambridge, MA: National Bureau of Economic Research, 2001.

Riemer M, Bickman L. "Using Program Theory to Link Social Psychology and Program Evaluation." In *Social Psychology and Evaluation.* M Mark, S Donaldson, and B Campbell (eds.). New York: Guilford Press, 2011, pp. 104–140.

Rossi PH, Lipsey MW, Freeman HE. *Evaluation: A Systematic Approach.* Thousand Oaks, CA: Sage Publications, 2004.

Smith SW, Daunic AP, Taylor GG. "Treatment Fidelity in Applied Educational Research: Expanding the Adoption and Application of Measures to Ensure Evidence-Based Practices." *Education and Treatment of Children*, 2007, 30 (4): 121–134.

Tanielian T, Jaycox LH. *Invisible Wounds of War: Psychological and Cognitive Injuries, Their Consequences, and Services to Assist Recovery.* Santa Monica, CA: RAND Corporation, MG-720-CCF, 2008. As of November 22, 2011:
http://www.rand.org/pubs/monographs/MG720.html

Trevisan MS, Huang YM. "Evaluability Assessment: A Primer." *Practical Assessment, Research & Evaluation*, 2003, 8 (20). As of October 24, 2011:
http://PAREonline.net/getvn.asp?v=8&n=20

U.S. Department of Veterans Affairs Office of Public Health and Environmental Hazards. "Analysis of VA Health Care Utilization Among Operation Enduring Freedom (OEF) and Operation Iraqi Freedom (OIF) Veterans." Presentation citing the *CTS Deployment File Baseline Report*, from the Defense Manpower Data Center, provided to the Environmental Epidemiology Service of the U.S. Department of Veterans Affairs Office of Public Health and Environmental Hazards by the Armed Force Health Surveillance Center, December 6, 2010.

U.S. Government Accountability Office. *Performance Measurement and Evaluation: Definitions and Relationships.* Publication No. GAO-05-739SP, May 2005. As of October 24, 2011:
http://www.gao.gov/special.pubs/gg98026.pdf

Weinick RM, Beckjord EB, Farmer CM, Martin LT, Gillen EM, Acosta JD, Fisher MP, Garnett J, Gonzalez G, Helmus TC, Jaycox LH, Reynolds KA, Salcedo N, Scharf DM. *Programs Addressing Psychological Health and Care for Traumatic Brain Injury Among U.S. Military Servicemembers and Their Families.* Santa Monica, CA: RAND Corporation, TR-950-OSD, 2011. As of November 22, 2011:
http://www.rand.org/pubs/technical_reports/TR950.html

Wholey JS. "Assessing the Feasibility and Likely Usefulness of Evaluation." In *Handbook of Practical Program Evaluation.* JS Wholey, HP Hatry, and KE Newcomer (eds.). San Francisco: Jossey-Bass, 1994, pp. 15–39.

Wholey JS. *Evaluation: Promise and Performance.* Washington, DC: The Urban Institute, 1979.

Wholey JS. "Using Evaluation to Improve Program Performance." In *Evaluation Research and Practice: Comparative and International Perspectives.* RA Levine, MA Solomon, G-M Hellstern, and H Wollmann (eds.). Beverly Hills, CA: Sage, 1981.

Wholey JS, Hatry HP, Newcomer KE (eds.). *Handbook of Practical Program Evaluation*, Vol. 19. San Francisco: Jossey-Bass, 2010.

Wilson SJ, Lipsey MW. "School-Based Interventions for Aggressive and Disruptive Behavior: Update of a Meta-Analysis." *American Journal of Preventive Medicine*, 2007, 33: 130–143.